2cc
9.21

10 Commandments
Family Nights Tool Chest

Creating Lasting Impressions for the Next Generation!

Jim Weidmann and John Warner
with Kurt Bruner

Cook Communications

Heritage™ Builders

This book is dedicated to my children, Nikki and Skylar Warner. In my opinion, the best kids that a dad could desire. Thank you for loving and teaching me so much! My wife, Gail, whose gifts of beauty, patience, and faith are a daily inspiration. Dad and Mom, Arch and Doris Warner, who taught me about parenting through love, constant encouragement, spiritual strength, being there, and going to church . . . every Sunday! As well, the memory of a dear friend, Jeff Foster, whose life has made a difference. His memory lives.

Thank You, Father, for all of the above. I am a blessed man!
—John Warner

Chariot Victor Publishing
a division of Cook Communications Ministries, Colorado Springs, Colorado 80918
Cook Communications, Paris, Ontario
Kingsway Communcations, Eastbourne, England

HERITAGE BUILDERS®/FAMILY NIGHT TOOL CHEST—TEN COMMANDMENTS™
© 1999 by Jim Weidmann, John Warner, and Kurt Bruner

First edition 1999

Edited by Steve Parolini
Design by Bill Gray
Interior Layout by Pat Miller
Cover and Interior Illustrations by Guy Wolek

ISBN 1-56476-780-9

Printed and bound in the United States of America
03 02 01 00   5 4 3 2

Heritage Builders/Family Night Tool Chest—Ten Commandments is a Heritage Builders® book.
To contact Heritage Builders Association, send email to: Hbuilders@aol.com.

Contents

Family Nights for the Ten Commandments

The Heritage Builders™ Series

This resource was created as an outreach of the Heritage Builders Association—a network of families and churches committed to passing a strong heritage to the next generation. Designed to motivate and assist families as they become intentional about the heritage passing process, this series draws upon the collective wisdom of parents, grandparents, church leaders, and family life experts, in an effort to provide balanced, biblical parenting advice along with effective, practical tools for family living. For more information on the goals and work of Heritage Builders Association, please see page 113.

Kurt Bruner, M.A.
Executive Editor
Heritage Builders® Series

@ Introduction

There is toothpaste all over the plastic-covered table. Four young kids are having the time of their lives squeezing the paste out of the tube—trying to expunge every drop like Dad told them to. "Okay," says Dad, slapping a twenty-dollar bill onto the table. "The first person to get the toothpaste back into their tube gets this money!" Little hands begin working to shove the peppermint pile back into rolled-up tubes—with very limited success.

Jim is in the midst of a weekly routine in the Weidmann home when he and his wife spend time creating "impression points" with the kids. "We can't do it, Dad!" protests the youngest child.

"The Bible tells us that's just like your tongue. Once the words come out, it's impossible to get them back in. You need to be careful what you say because you may wish you could take it back." An unforgettable impression is made.

Impression points occur every day of our lives. Intentionally or not, we impress upon our children our values, preferences, beliefs, quirks, and concerns. It happens both through our talk and through our walk. When we do it right, we can turn them on to the things we believe. But when we do it wrong, we can turn them off to the values we most hope they will embrace. The goal is to find ways of making this reality work for us, rather than against us. How? By creating and capturing opportunities to impress upon the next generation our values and beliefs. In other words, through what we've labeled impression points.

The kids are all standing at the foot of the stairs. Jim is at the top of that same staircase. They wait eagerly for Dad's instructions.

"I'll take you to Baskin Robbins for ice cream if you can figure how to get up here." He has the attention of all four kids. "But there are a few rules. First, you can't touch the stairs. Second, you can't touch the railing. Now, begin!"

After several contemplative moments, the youngest speaks up. "That's impossible, Dad! How can we get to where you are without touching the stairs or the railing?"

After some disgruntled agreement from two of the other children, Jacob gets an idea. "Hey, Dad. Come down here." Jim walks down the stairs. "Now bend over while I get on your back. Okay, climb the stairs."

Bingo! Jim proceeds to parallel this simple game with how it is impossible to get to God on our own. But when we trust Christ's completed work on our behalf, we can get to heaven. A lasting impression is made. After a trip up the stairs on Dad's back, the whole gang piles into the minivan for a double scoop of mint-chip.

Several years ago, Jim and his wife Janet began setting aside time to intentionally impress upon the kids their values and beliefs through a weekly ritual called "family night." They play games, talk, study, and do the things which reinforce the importance of family and faith. It is during these times that they intentionally create these impression points with their kids. The impact? The kids are having fun and a heritage is being passed.

☙ intentional or "oops"?

Sometimes, we accidentally impress the wrong things on our kids rather than intentionally impressing the right things. But there is an effective, easy way to change that. Routine family nights are a powerful tool for creating intentional impression points with our children.

The concept behind family nights is rooted in a biblical mandate summarized in Deuteronomy 6:5-9.

> *"Love the LORD your God with all your heart and with all your soul and with all your strength. These commandments that I give you today are to be upon your hearts. Impress them on your children."*
> *How?*
> *"Talk about them when you sit at home and when you walk along the road, when you lie down and when you get up. Tie them as symbols on your hands and bind them on your foreheads. Write them on the doorframes of your houses and on your gates."*

In other words, we need to take advantage of every opportunity to impress our beliefs and values in the lives of our children. A growing network of parents are discovering family nights to be a highly effective, user-friendly approach to doing just that. As one father put it, "This has changed our entire family life." And another dad, "Our investment of time and energy into family nights has more eternal value than we may ever know." Why? Because they are intentionally teaching their children at the wisdom level, the level at which the children understand and can apply eternal truths.

☙ truth is a treasure

Two boys are running all over the house, carefully following the complex and challenging instructions spelled out on the "truth treasure map" they received moments ago. An earlier map contained a few rather simple instructions that were much easier to follow. But the "false treasure box" it lead to left something to be desired. It was empty. Boo Dad! They hope for a better result with map number two.

STEP ONE:

Walk sixteen paces into the front family room.

STEP TWO:

Spin around seven times, then walk down the stairs.

STEP THREE:

Run backwards to the other side of the room.

STEP FOUR:

Try and get around Dad and climb under the table.

You get the picture. The boys are laughing at themselves, complaining to Dad, and having a ball. After twenty minutes of treasure hunting they finally reach the elusive "truth treasure box." Little hands open the lid, hoping for a better result this time around. They aren't disappointed. The box contains a nice selection of their favorite candies. Yea Dad!

"Which map was easier to follow?" Dad asks.

"The first one," comes their response.

"Which one was better?"

"The second one. It led to a true treasure," says the oldest.

"That's just like life," Dad shares. "Sometimes it's easier to follow what is false. But it is always better to seek and follow what is true."

They read from Proverbs 2 about the hidden treasure of God's truth and end their time repeating tonight's jingle—"It's best for you to seek what's true." Then they indulge themselves with a mouthful of delicious candy!

℮ the power of family nights

The power of family nights is twofold. First, it creates a formal setting within which Dad and Mom can intentionally instill beliefs, values, or character qualities within their child. Rather than defer to the influence of peers and media, or abdicate character training to the school and church, parents create the opportunity to teach their children the things that matter most.

The second impact of family nights is perhaps even more significant than the first. Twenty to sixty minutes of formal fun and instruction can set up countless opportunities for informal reinforcement. These informal impression points do not have to be created, they just happen—at the dinner table, while driving in the car, while watching television, or any other parent/child time together. Once you have formally discussed a given family night topic, you and your children will naturally refer back to those principles during the routine dialogues of everyday life.

If the truth were known, many of us hated family devotions while growing up. We had them sporadically at best, usually whenever our parents were feeling particularly guilty. But that was fine, since the only thing worse was a trip to the dentist. Honestly, do we really think that is what God had in mind when He instructed us to teach our children? As an alternative, many parents are discovering family nights to be a wonderful complement to or replacement for family devotions as a means of passing their beliefs and values to the kids. In fact, many parents hear their kids ask at least three times per week:

"Can we have family night tonight?"

Music to Dad's and Mom's ears!

⊙ Keys to Effective Family Nights

There are several keys which should be incorporated into effective family nights.

MAKE IT FUN!

Enjoy yourself, and let the kids have a ball. They may not remember everything you say, but they will always cherish the times of laughter—and so will you.

KEEP IT SIMPLE!

The minute you become sophisticated or complicated, you've missed the whole point. Don't try to create deeply profound lessons. Just try to reinforce your values and beliefs in a simple, easy-to-understand manner. Read short passages, not long, drawn-out sections of Scripture. Remember: The goal is to keep it simple.

DON'T DOMINATE!

You want to pull them into the discovery process as much as possible. If you do all the talking, you've missed the mark. Ask questions, give assignments, invite participation in every way possible. They will learn more when you involve all of their senses and emotions.

GO WITH THE FLOW!

It's fine to start with a well-defined outline, but don't kill spontaneity by becoming overly structured. If an incident or question leads you in a different direction, great! Some of the best impression opportunities are completely unplanned and unexpected.

MIX IT UP!

Don't allow yourself to get into a rut or routine. Keep the sense of excitement and anticipation through variety. Experiment to discover what works best for your family. Use books, games, videos, props, made-up stories, songs, music or music videos, or even go on a family outing.

DO IT OFTEN!

We tend to find time for the things that are really important. It is best to set aside one evening per week (the same evening if possible) for family night. Remember, repetition is the best teacher. The more impressions you can create, the more of an impact you will make.

MAKE A MEMORY!

Find ways to make the lesson stick. For example, just as advertisers create "jingles" to help us remember their products, it is helpful to create family night "jingles" to remember the main theme—such as "It's best for you to seek what's true" or "Just like air, God is there!"

USE OTHER TOOLS FROM THE HERITAGE BUILDERS TOOL CHEST!

Family night is only one exciting way for you to intentionally build a loving heritage for your family. You'll also want to use these other exciting tools from Heritage Builders.

The Family Fragrance: There are five key qualities to a healthy family fragrance, each contributing to an environment of love in the home. It's easy to remember the Fragrance Five by fitting them into an acrostic using the word "Aroma"—

> A—Affection
> R—Respect
> O—Order
> M—Merriment
> A—Affirmation

Impression Points: Ways that we impress on our children our values, preferences, and concerns. We do it through our talk and our actions. We do it intentionally (through such methods as Family Nights), and we do it incidentally.

The Family Compass: The Family Compass is the standard of normal healthy living against which our children will be able to measure their atttitudes, actions, and beliefs.

Traditions: Meaningful activities which promote the process of passing on emotional, spiritual, and relational inheritance between generations. Family traditions can play a vital role in this process.

Please see the back of the book for information on how to receive the FREE Heritage Builders Newsletter which contains more information about these exciting tools! Also, look for the new book, *The Heritage,* available at your local Christian bookstore.

How to Use This Tool Chest

Summary page: For those who like the bottom line, we have provided a summary sheet at the start of each family night session. This abbreviated version of the topic briefly highlights the goal, key Scriptures, activity overview, main points, and life slogan. On the reverse side of this detachable page there is space provided for you to write down any ideas you wish to add or alter as you make the lesson your own.

Step-by-step: For those seeking suggestions and directions for each step in the family night process, we have provided a section which walks you through every activity, question, Scripture reading, and discussion point. Feel free to follow each step as written as you conduct the session, or read through this portion in preparation for your time together.

À la carte: We strongly encourage you to use the material in this book in an "à la carte" manner. In other words, pick and choose the questions, activities, Scriptures, age-appropriate ideas, etc. which best fit your family. This book is not intended to serve as a curriculum, requiring compliance with our sequence and plan, but rather as a tool chest from which you can grab what works for you and which can be altered to fit your family situation.

The long and the short of it: Each family night topic presented in this book includes several activities, related Scriptures, and possible discussion items. Do not feel it is necessary to conduct them all in a single family night. You may wish to spread one topic over several weeks using smaller portions of each chapter, depending upon the attention span of the kids and the energy level of the parents. Remember, short and effective is better than long and thorough.

Journaling: Finally, we have provided space with each session for you to capture a record of meaningful comments, funny happenings, and unplanned moments which will inevitably occur during family night. Keep a notebook of these journal entries for future reference. You will treasure this permanent record of the heritage passing process for years to come.

⊚ 1: The Importance of the Ten Commandments

Teaching children the importance of the Ten Commandments as a target for righteous living

Scripture
- Exodus 20:3-17
- Romans 3:20; 7:7-20

ACTIVITY OVERVIEW		
Activity	Summary	Pre-Session Prep
Activity 1: Bean Bag Toss	Toss bean bags and discuss why we must shoot for the target of obeying the Ten Commandments.	You'll need a target with 10 holes, balls, bean bags or rolled socks to throw at target.
Activity 2: Measuring	Explore how the Ten Commandments help us see how we're "measuring up" to the way God would have us live.	You'll need butcher paper, pens, measuring tape, and a Bible.

Main Points:

—The Ten Commandments are the standards for how God wants us to live.

—The Ten Commandments show us our sinfulness and our need for a Savior.

LIFE SLOGAN: "God gave the big ten to guide all men."

Make it your own
In the space provided below, outline the flow and add any additional ideas to guide you through the process of conducting this family night.

Prayer & Praise Items
In the space provided below, list any items you wish to pray about or give praise for during this family night session.

Journal
In the space provided below, capture a record of any fun or meaningful things which happened during this family night session.

Session Tip

We intentionally have provided more material than we would expect to be used in a single "Family Night" session. You know your family's unique interests and life circumstances best, so feel free to adapt this lesson to meet your family members' needs. Remember, short and simple is better than long and comprehensive.

WARM-UP

Open with Prayer: Begin by having a family member pray, asking God to help everyone in the family understand more about Him through this time. After prayer, review your last lesson by asking these questions:

- **What did we learn about in our last lesson?**
- **What was the Life Slogan?**
- **Have your actions changed because of what we learned? If so, how?** Encourage family members to give specific examples of how they've applied learning from the past week.

Share: Today we're going to learn about why God gave us the Ten Commandments.

ACTIVITY 1: Bean Bag Toss

Point: The Ten Commandments are the standards for how God wants us to live.

Supplies: You'll need a target with 10 holes, and balls, bean bags or rolled socks to throw at the target.

Activity: Prepare your target by cutting 10 various-sized holes in a large sheet of cardboard or in the bottom of a large box. Make sure each of the holes is big enough for a ball or bean bag to fall through. Mark a number (from one to 10) next to each hole, representing the number of points for that hole. You may wish to have your children help you create the target and decorate it.

Set the target up in a large room that is free from breakable items. Mark a "tossing line" a few feet from the box.

Give each family member a chance to make 10 tosses at the target, attempting to get the ball or bean bag into one of the holes. Add the total of the points scored for each family member and reward the winner with a big family hug. Then reward everyone else with a big hug too just for trying their best!

 Then ask:

- **What was it like to try and hit the target in this game?** (It was hard; I did pretty well; I kept missing.)

Share: Trying to hit the targets and score lots of points isn't always easy. After God led Moses and the Israelites out of Egypt, they were having a hard time "hitting a target" too. But their target was the target of following God. They kept missing the holes and making bad choices. The Ten Commandments were given to Moses to share with the Israelites. These Ten Commandments are ten rules for living.

- **Why do you think God gave the Ten Commandments to the people?** (It gave the people a clear understanding of how God wanted them to live; it helped them know what decisions to make; it helped them hit the target.)
- **Do you think that the Ten Commandments apply to us today?** (Yes, God's expectations for us are the same as for the people of Moses' time; God's commandments are so clear, simple and exact that they still apply.)
- **Look at the Ten Commandments (Exodus 20:3-17) and tell me what you notice about the first four and the last six.** (The first four tell us about God and the last six tell us how we are to love one another.)

Share: God wanted His people to "hit the target" and learn to follow God. That's why He gave the Israelites (and us) the Ten Commandments. God wants us to aim to live a life of obedience because we love God. He wants us to follow the Ten Commandments because He knows what's best for us and wants us to love Him more and treat others with love.

Age Adjustments

Make sure to adjust the tossing distance for each family member during this activity. Allow younger children to toss from just a couple feet away from the target. Have older children (and parents) step back quite a ways so each family member has an equal chance of scoring lots of points.

ACTIVITY 2: Measuring

Point: The Ten Commandments show us our sinfulness and our need for a Savior.

 Supplies: You'll need butcher paper, pens, measuring tape, and a Bible.

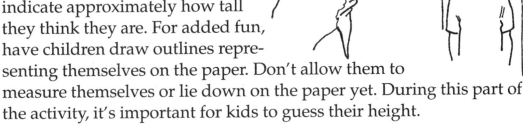

Activity: Lay butcher paper on the floor. Have children take turns making marks on the paper to indicate approximately how tall they think they are. For added fun, have children draw outlines representing themselves on the paper. Don't allow them to measure themselves or lie down on the paper yet. During this part of the activity, it's important for kids to guess their height.

 When each child has drawn an outline or marked their height, ask:

- **How close do you think you came to your actual height?** (Very close; not close at all.)

Have children take turns lying down on the butcher paper while you mark their actual height next to their guesses. Then have children look at the difference between their first guess and the actual height.

Ask children to guess how many inches tall they are. List that number next to their outline. Then have them help you use a measuring tape to find out their true height. Once again, compare the guess to the actual height.

 Then ask:

- **How close were you to guessing the right height or making the right marks on the paper?** (I was off by a lot; I was pretty close.)

 Read Romans 3:20 and 7:7-20. Then ask:

- **What is sin?** (Disobeying God; missing the mark; making wrong choices.)
- **How is the way we missed the mark in measuring ourselves like the way we miss the mark in our relationship with God?** (We can't do everything on our own; we mess up even in small things.)

Share: The Ten Commandments reveal to us how we miss the mark for the way God wants us to live. It shows us that we need to repent (confess) to restore our fellowship with God.

Spend a little time in prayer together, thanking God for the Ten Commandments and asking for forgiveness for the times when you've messed up and not followed the Ten Commandments or have sinned in other ways.

WRAP-UP

Gather everyone in a circle and have family members take turns answering this question: **What's one thing you've learned about God today?**

Next, tell kids you've got a new "Life Slogan" you'd like to share with them.

Life Slogan: Today's Life Slogan is this: "God gave the big ten to guide all men." Have family members repeat the slogan two or three times to help them learn it. Then encourage them to practice saying it during the week so they can talk about it at your next family night session.

Close in Prayer: Allow time for each family member to share prayer concerns and answers to prayer. Then close your time together with prayer for each concern. Thank God for listening to and caring about us.

Remember to record your prayer requests so you can refer to them in the future as you see God answering them.

℮ 2: Why the Ten Commandments Are Relevant Today

Teaching children the importance of the Ten Commandments and to "call sin—sin"

Scripture
• Exodus 20

ACTIVITY OVERVIEW		
Activity	Summary	Pre-Session Prep
Activity 1: Picture This	Play a game and learn what it means to name something for what it truly is.	You'll need paper, pens or pencils, and a Bible.
Activity 2: Shadow Plays	Learn how obedience is a result of loving God, not a reason to love God.	You'll need a light source and a variety of objects (see the lesson for examples).

Main Points:

—The Ten Commandments help us to identify what sin is in today's world.

—Because we love God, we obey His commandments.

LIFE SLOGAN: "Call sin—sin, don't enter in."

Make it your own

In the space provided below, outline the flow and add any additional ideas to guide you through the process of conducting this family night.

Prayer & Praise Items

In the space provided below, list any items you wish to pray about or give praise for during this family night session.

Journal

In the space provided below, capture a record of any fun or meaningful things which happened during this family night session.

WARM-UP

Open with Prayer: Begin by having a family member pray, asking God to help everyone in the family understand more about Him through this time. After prayer, review your last lesson by asking these questions:

- **What did we learn about in our last lesson?**
- **What was the Life Slogan?**
- **Have your actions changed because of what we learned? If so, how?** Encourage family members to give specific examples of how they've applied learning from the past week.

Share: Today we're going to learn what it means to "call sin—sin" and how the Ten Commandments help us see what is right and wrong.

ACTIVITY 1: Picture This

Point: The Ten Commandments help us to identify what sin is in today's world.

 Supplies: You'll need paper, pens or pencils, and a Bible.

Activity: Prepare a list of words that can be used in this variation of "Pictionary." Here are a few suggested words:

Rock	House
Boat	Bed
Chair	Skyscraper
Parrot	Bulldozer
Beaver	Reindeer

Have children take turns drawing objects from your word list. Have other family members attempt to guess the object as quickly as possible. Give more difficult words to older children and simpler ones to younger children. Play a number of rounds so each person gets a chance to draw and to guess at least three times. Parents say "no" every time there is a wrong guess at the object being drawn.

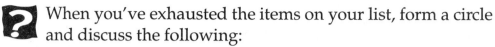 When you've exhausted the items on your list, form a circle and discuss the following:
- **What did you like about this game?** (Guessing the objects; drawing pictures.)
- **What did it take to win this game?** (We had to name the objects that were drawn.)
- **What was it like when you guessed the wrong name?** (I was sad; I felt bad; I didn't win.)

Share: It's fun to play a game like this and call out the right names for objects. But in today's world, people often call things by the wrong name on purpose. They do this so they don't have to deal with the consequences.

Discuss some of the following examples of how people call things by different names for the sake of explaining them away or not taking responsibility for the true nature of the issue. Choose examples that are appropriate to the ages of your children.

When you hurt someone's feelings = you say, "Just teasing!"
When you are mean to someone in front of others = you say, "Just having fun!"
Pornography = free speech
Abortion = free choice
Homosexuality = diversity
Lying = eating off the salad bar on Mom's ticket or staying at a hotel free because even though you're 13, you look 12 years old
Cheating = copying someone's homework and saying it's yours and they just helped you

Have children suggest other examples of how people explain away things that are wrong with fancy words or excuses.

Read aloud the Ten Commandments (found in Ex. 20). Then, as a family, list as many sins as you can that "fit" under each of the commandments.

Age Adjustments

OLDER CHILDREN AND TEENAGERS will have a keen interest in the concepts presented in this activity. Calling something by its true name is often a point of contention for teenagers—many of whom would prefer to excuse actions and words rather than accept responsibility for poor choices. Help your older children examine how they deal with sins that others might just as easily explain away as "not wrong at all." Use this activity to spark thoughtful discussion about calling sin—sin and what that means for a teenager who is always under the scrutiny of peers.

 Then ask:

- **What does the world use for its standard?** (Whatever it wants; whatever the most people agree on; wrong things.)
- **What is our standard for living?** (God's Word; God's teaching as found in the Bible.)

Share: The world tells us that it's okay to do things that are wrong and uses excuses to explain why it's okay. But the Bible tells us it's important to call sin—sin, and to follow God's teaching. The Ten Commandments help us to follow God's teaching and remind us of things that are sin. When we follow the Ten Commandments, we are following what God wants us to do.

ACTIVITY 2: Shadow Plays

Point: Because we love God, we obey His commands.

 Supplies: You'll need a light source and a variety of objects (such as: stuffed animals, a spoon, a bottle, a shoe, a television remote control, a pair of glasses, and so on—be creative).

Activity: Set up a light source somewhere in a room where you can cast shadows on a plain wall (or a sheet of newsprint taped to the wall). Have children sit near the wall, but in front of the light source so they won't be able to see what you're holding up to the light.

One at a time, hold up different objects so they cast shadows on the wall. Have children take turns guessing what the objects are. Have fun with the items you choose and be sure to include some that might be difficult to guess.

 Then ask:

- **What did you see on the wall?** (Kids may list the actual objects they saw or explain that they saw shadows.)
- **How was the shadow similar to the actual object?** (It was the same shape; it looked like it; it was the same size.)
- **How was it different?** (It was just a shadow; it wasn't the item at all; you couldn't pick it up.)

Share: The shadow was created by the object, but it wasn't the object. In the same way, our obedience is not love but only a reflection of our love for God. People who obey the Ten Commandments may or may not love God. But people who love God will know that it is important to reflect that love by obeying Him. Our obedience comes out of our love.

Age Adjustments

YOUNGER CHILDREN may have a difficult time understanding this concept. To make it simpler, ask younger children why they choose to obey you. They'll likely answer, "because that's what you want me to do" or "because I love you." Both of these answers can then be applied to the way we're to relate to God. When children see how their relationship with their Heavenly Father can be compared to their relationship with their earthly parents, they begin to understand the weightier aspects of what it means to be a Christian.

WRAP-UP

Gather everyone in a circle and have family members take turns answering this question: **What's one thing you've learned about God today?**

Next, tell kids you've got a new "Life Slogan" you'd like to share with them.

Life Slogan: Today's Life Slogan is this: "Call sin—sin, don't enter in." Have family members repeat the slogan two or three times to help them learn it. Then encourage them to practice saying it during the week so they can talk about it at your next family night session.

Close in Prayer: Allow time for each family member to share prayer concerns and answers to prayer. Then close your time together with prayer for each concern. Thank God for listening to and caring about us.

Remember to record your prayer requests so you can refer to them in the future as you see God answering them.

☺ 3: The First Commandment
You shall have no other gods before Me

Teaching children that God is the one true God

Scripture
- Exodus 20:3
- Matthew 4:10

ACTIVITY OVERVIEW		
Activity	Summary	Pre-Session Prep
Activity 1: One True God	Learn how people are sometimes fooled into believing false gods.	You'll need small cups that look identical (such as Dixie cups), a small object (such as a ball), and a Bible.
Activity 2: Priorities	Discover how they spend their time now, and how they could spend more time with God.	You'll need 24 dominoes or small blocks for each family member, and a Bible.

Main Points:

—There is only one true God we can trust and believe in.

—We should live God-centered lives.

LIFE SLOGAN: "You shall have no other gods before Me."

Make it your own
In the space provided below, outline the flow and add any additional ideas to guide you through the process of conducting this family night.

Prayer & Praise Items
In the space provided below, list any items you wish to pray about or give praise for during this family night session.

Journal
In the space provided below, capture a record of any fun or meaningful things which happened during this family night session.

Session Tip

We intentionally have provided more material than we would expect to be used in a single "Family Night" session. You know your family's unique interests and life circumstances best, so feel free to adapt this lesson to meet your family members' needs. Remember, short and simple is better than long and comprehensive.

 WARM-UP

Open with Prayer: Begin by having a family member pray, asking God to help everyone in the family understand more about Him through this time. After prayer, review your last lesson by asking these questions:

- **What did we learn about in our last lesson?**
- **What was the Life Slogan?**
- **Have your actions changed because of what we learned? If so, how?** Encourage family members to give specific examples of how they've applied learning from the past week.

Share: Today we're going to learn about the first commandment: You shall have no other gods before Me!

ACTIVITY 1: One True God

Point: There is only one true God we can trust and believe in.

Supplies: You'll need small cups that look identical (such as Dixie cups), a small object (such as a ball), and a Bible.

Activity: Place a small ball on a table. Then cover the ball with one of the identical cups and place the other two cups on either side of this cup. Play the "shell game" where you slide the cups around the table in random fashion, mixing things up so family members have a difficult time keeping up with the location of the cup that covers the ball.

After mixing up the cups, have volunteers guess which cup is covering the ball. Repeat this activity numerous times, speeding up your

Age Adjustments

In this day of pluralism and "anything goes" theology, OLDER CHILDREN AND TEENAGERS should be equipped to recognize and understand how the Christian view of God differs from other views. Use the following acrostic to help your children easily summarize the six primary views of God. Once learned, refer back to this exercise as you recognize a different view of God as you watch films, read books, encounter people of different faiths, etc. The main views of God can be summarized using the acrostic "FAMOUS" as follows.

LETTER	TITLE	SUMMARY
F	Force god	see below
A	Accident god	see below
M	Man god	see below
O	Our God	see below
U	Up There god	see below
S	Swing god	see below

"FORCE GOD" SUMMARY

NEW AGE PANTHEISM: This view says God is an impersonal force rather than a personal being, much like the force of the *Star Wars* films.

"ACCIDENT GOD" SUMMARY

ATHEISM: This view says there is no god, so everything that exists came about by accident with no creator.

"MAN GOD" SUMMARY

POLYTHEISM/MORMONISM: This view says that as man is, God once was—and as God is, man shall become. It is a form of polytheism—the belief in many gods.

"OUR GOD" SUMMARY

CHRISTIAN THEISM: This view says that God created us, loves us, and came down to us to die for our sins and rise from the dead so that we can be with Him.

"UP THERE GOD" SUMMARY

JUDAISM/ISLAM: This view says that God created us, but did not come down to us. He instead stayed "up there" and expects us to work our way to Him.

"SWING GOD" SUMMARY

DEISM: This view says that God created everything and set up the natural laws, but is not involved with human affairs. Like a swing, He pushed it to get it started, but has left it alone since.

cup mixing so family members occasionally guess wrong. Then have family members take turns mixing up the cups, trying to trick you into guessing incorrectly.

 After you've enjoyed this game for a while, discuss these questions:

• **What made it hard to know which cup was covering the ball?** (The cups looked alike; I couldn't keep track of where the ball was.)

• **If we call the ball, "Truth," how is this game like the way people make choices in real life?** (People look for truth in the wrong place; the truth is hard to find sometimes.)

Share: Trying to find the ball among the three cups is kind of like trying to find the truth when you don't have a relationship with the one true God. People who don't know God or who believe in other gods are constantly guessing wrong about the truth and about decisions in life. Some trust in their ability to make money, some in money itself, some put their trust in other people. But all of these things will someday fail: Money can't buy you health; material goods can't pay your bills; other peoples' expectations will change.

But God promises and delivers. He will never leave us nor forsake us; He knows what is best for us better than we do; He has given us eternal life; and He answers our prayers.

 Read aloud Exodus 20:3. **Share: The first of the Ten Command-ments reminds us that there is only one true God. All other places we seek truth will end up being empty. Only God can fill our needs and lead us to eternal life.**

ACTIVITY 2: Priorities

Point: We should live God-centered lives.

Supplies: You'll need 24 dominoes or small blocks for each family member, and a Bible.

Activity: Give each family member 24 dominoes or blocks. Then have family members each separate their dominoes into piles based on how they spend their time in a typical day. For example, someone might stack up 2 blocks to represent eating time, 8 blocks to represent sleeping time, 4 hours to represent play time, and so on.

? Then ask:
- **What is the greatest command God gave?** (Love the Lord with all your heart; love God first.)
- **How do your dominoes represent that command in your life?** (They don't; I spend lots of time with God; I don't spend a lot of time worshiping or praying.)
- **What can you do to give more time to God?** (Spend time reading the Bible; pray more often.)

Age Adjustments

OLDER CHILDREN AND TEENAGERS may want to write out "commitment contracts" outlining their plans for making God the center of their lives. These contracts might list specific things they'll do to grow closer to God and delineate the time they plan on spending with God. Help them make realistic goals, so they can feel successful in their efforts to grow closer to God.

Have family members rearrange the dominoes to give more time to God if they're lacking in this area (many won't have any pile at all dedicated to growing closer to God). Don't pressure kids, but allow them to think through the current priorities as represented by their domino piles and come up with an idea for giving God more time.

Share: We can give God more time by reading the Bible, praying often, having a quiet time to listen to God, and even by asking, "What would Jesus do?" every time we have to make a difficult decision. God wants to be the center of our lives.

Read aloud Matthew 4:10. Then **share: There is only one true God, and He wants us to get to know Him better each day. Let us each find ways to give more "domino" time to God in the weeks to come.**

Have children place their dominoes in their bedrooms as reminders of their desire to make God the center of their lives. Take time to pray, asking God to help each family member spend more time with Him.

WRAP-UP

Gather everyone in a circle and have family members take turns answering this question: **What's one thing you've learned about God today?**

Next, tell kids you've got a new "Life Slogan" you'd like to share with them.

Life Slogan: Today's Life Slogan is this: "You shall have no other gods before Me." Have family members repeat the slogan two or three times to help them learn it. Then encourage them to practice saying it during the week so they can talk about it at your next family night session.

Close in Prayer: Allow time for each family member to share prayer concerns and answers to prayer. Then close your time together with prayer for each concern. Thank God for listening to and caring about us.

Remember to record your prayer requests so you can refer to them in the future as you see God answering them.

🌀 4: The Second Commandment
You shall not make for yourself an idol

Teaching children the value of not worshiping idols

Scripture
- Exodus 20:4-6
- Isaiah 46:1-11
- Colossians 3:5-6

ACTIVITY OVERVIEW		
Activity	Summary	Pre-Session Prep
Activity 1: Idol Thinking	Discover how earthly idols can't replace the love God has for them.	You'll need various items representing your children's favorite media stars and a Bible.
Activity 2: Not Just Wood and Stone	Learn how different things can become idols, and how to put God first.	Have children bring a "favorite thing" to this activity and a Bible.

Main Points:

— Only God can provide for our needs.

— Idols come in all shapes and sizes.

LIFE SLOGAN: "You shall not make for yourself an idol."

Make it your own

In the space provided below, outline the flow and add any additional ideas to guide you through the process of conducting this family night.

Prayer & Praise Items

In the space provided below, list any items you wish to pray about or give praise for during this family night session.

Journal

In the space provided below, capture a record of any fun or meaningful things which happened during this family night session.

Session Tip

We intentionally have provided more material than we would expect to be used in a single "Family Night" session. You know your family's unique interests and life circumstances best, so feel free to adapt this lesson to meet your family members' needs. Remember, short and simple is better than long and comprehensive.

 WARM-UP

Open with Prayer: Begin by having a family member pray, asking God to help everyone in the family understand more about Him through this time. After prayer, review your last lesson by asking these questions:

• **What did we learn about in our last lesson?**
• **What was the Life Slogan?**
• **Have your actions changed because of what we learned? If so, how?** Encourage family members to give specific examples of how they've applied learning from the past week.

Share: Today we're going to learn about the second commandment: You shall not make for yourself an idol.

ACTIVITY 1: Idol Thinking

Point: Only God can provide for our needs.

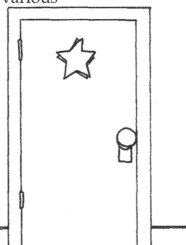 **Supplies:** You'll need a Bible and various items representing your children's favorite media stars. This could include posters, CDs, videos, and any other items your child owns. You may even wish to rent a video (if the media star has a recent, age-appropriate video available).

Activity: Play a video and/or a CD of your child(ren)'s idolized media star. After allowing time to listen to the song or view a portion of the star's video, turn off the TV or the CD player and discuss the following:

- **What makes this person/band so special to you?** (I like the way he/she sings; I like the movies this person has been in; I just think this person is cool.) (The answers to this question will vary greatly, but the importance of this activity is to open up an abundance of dialogue. Encourage your children to describe in as much detail as possible, what makes the media star so important to them. You may wish to list these reasons on a sheet of paper or newsprint for all to see.)
- **Do you think that (this media star) spends the same amount of time "idolizing" you, as you spend idolizing him or her?** (No.)

- **What, if anything, does this media star know about you?** (Nothing; probably just my name because I sent him fan mail.)
- **How much interest would your media star idol have in you if you were sick or had a broken arm? If your pet died?** (Not much; none; probably a little if he or she knew me.)

Age Adjustments

YOUNGER CHILDREN may have some difficulty understanding the concept of idols. You can help them connect with this important commandment by referring to an actual experience they've had recently, such as: wanting to play rather than pray at bedtime; whining about buying something with money that was designated for church; or choosing the television over family time. Help them see how the things around us (which can be good in moderation), can become as important as God and why this is wrong.

Take time to briefly discuss other idols people sometimes have. These could include: money; toys; food; friends; and much more.

Then **share: We've learned from this discussion that our media stars—our idols—don't care much about us; are powerless to fill our needs; and probably are unworthy of our praise. Does that mean it's wrong to look up to people like these? No. But when we put our faith in these people—or in the things we listed as idols— we're heading for disaster. Only God deserves our reverence and honor in this way.**

 Ask:

- **When your pet dies, or a friend hurts your feelings, or a family member is sick, do you ever turn to God and ask for His help? How can God comfort us in these times?** (He gives us peace; we can pray for Him to help us; He loves us.)

 Read aloud Exodus 20:4-6. Once again, summarize the commandment and emphasize that God is a God of His word.

ACTIVITY 2: Not Just Wood and Stone

Point: Idols come in all shapes and sizes.

 Supplies: Have children bring a "favorite thing" to this activity and a Bible.

Activity: Ask each child to demonstrate to everyone what the "favorite thing" is that he or she brought to the table. Your job as facilitator is to demonstrate to them that an "object" or a "thing" has no spirit or soul. It is completely unable to demonstrate any type of feelings or actions towards the one who "loves" it.

For instance, let's assume that your child brought a CD player. You might ask him or her the following:

- **How much time do you spend listening to/and honoring this daily?**
- **What kind of joy/satisfaction does this bring to you?**
- **How long do you think that this will last before it no longer works?**
- **Does this CD player initiate its operation by itself, or does it rely on you?**
- **How much time do you spend reading your Bible, praying, and being in fellowship with fellow Christians per week?**
- **How does that compare with the amount of time you spend with the CD player?**

Share: Idols of the Old Testament days were typically inanimate objects made out of stone, wood, or metal. But today's idols come in all shapes and sizes. The Babylonians had many gods, and their worship of these gods included terrible things such as child sacrifice. They had a god for every desire. What are some of today's idols?

- **Money—We strive to gain as much money as possible even when it hurts our families or those around us. Money becomes more important than anything.**
- **Material possessions—We love new toys, games, books, movies, cars, and all kinds of things. But sometimes, those things get more of our attention than God. When that happens, they become idols.**

 Read Isaiah 46:1-11.

Share: Isaiah tells us, "Who shapes a god and casts an idol, which can

profit him nothing?" We think of idols as statues of wood or stone, but in reality an idol is anything natural that is given sacred value and power. If your answer to any of the following questions is anything or anyone other than God, you may need to check out who or what you are worshiping.

- Who created me?
- Whom do I ultimately trust?
- Whom do I look to for ultimate truth?
- Whom do I look to for security and happiness?
- Who is in charge of my future?

 Read Colossians 3:5-6.

Share: God comforts us. God loves us. Idols can't. Let us commit to think about and give our love to God, not idols. When we love God and not idols, we are keeping the second commandment.

WRAP-UP

Gather everyone in a circle and have family members take turns answering this question: **What's one thing you've learned about God today?**

Next, tell kids you've got a new "Life Slogan" you'd like to share with them.

Life Slogan: Today's Life Slogan is this: "You shall not make for yourself an idol." Have family members repeat the slogan two or three times to help them learn it. Then encourage them to practice saying it during the week so they can talk about it at your next family night session.

Close in Prayer: Allow time for each family member to share prayer concerns and answers to prayer. Then close your time together with prayer for each concern. Thank God for listening to and caring about us.

Remember to record your prayer requests so you can refer to them in the future as you see God answering them.

5: Commandment Three
You shall not misuse the name of the Lord your God

Teaching children the importance of using God's name in holiness

Scripture
- Exodus 20:7
- Matthew 5:34
- Psalm 99:3

ACTIVITY OVERVIEW		
Activity	Summary	Pre-Session Prep
Activity 1: Fictionary	Play a game and learn the power and value of names.	You'll need a dictionary, pieces of paper, pencils, and a Bible.
Activity 2: Toss Carefully	Toss eggs back and forth and discuss why it's important to treat God's name with respect.	You'll need eggs, a checkbook, and a Bible.

Main Points:

—God's name represents His character, personage, nature, reputation, and role.

—We need to treat God's name with holiness for it represents God who is holy.

LIFE SLOGAN: "You shall not misuse the name of the Lord your God."

Make it your own

In the space provided below, outline the flow and add any additional ideas to guide you through the process of conducting this family night.

Prayer & Praise Items

In the space provided below, list any items you wish to pray about or give praise for during this family night session.

Journal

In the space provided below, capture a record of any fun or meaningful things which happened during this family night session.

Session Tip

We intentionally have provided more material than we would expect to be used in a single "Family Night" session. You know your family's unique interests and life circumstances best, so feel free to adapt this lesson to meet your family members' needs. Remember, short and simple is better than long and comprehensive.

WARM-UP

Open with Prayer: Begin by having a family member pray, asking God to help everyone in the family understand more about Him through this time. After prayer, review your last lesson by asking these questions:

- **What did we learn about in our last lesson?**
- **What was the Life Slogan?**
- **Have your actions changed because of what we learned? If so, how?** Encourage family members to give specific examples of how they've applied learning from the past week.

Share: Today we're going to learn about the third commandment: You shall not misuse the name of the Lord your God.

ACTIVITY 1: Fictionary

Point: God's name represents His character, personage, nature, reputation, and role.

Supplies: You'll need a dictionary, pieces of paper, pencils, and a Bible.

Activity: Open by playing a game of "fictionary" with your family. Here's how: Have someone choose an unfamiliar word from the dictionary and write it on a piece of paper. Then have other family members secretly write a definition for that word (it can be a serious attempt to guess the meaning, a humorous guess, or anything that might seem believable). Have the person who chose the word also write the real definition on a similar sheet of paper.

Then have the person who chose the word mix up the papers and randomly read each definition. Ask family members to each vote on one definition they think is correct. Award one point to the definition writer for each vote his or her fake definition received. Also, award one point to each person who chose the right definition. If no one guesses the correct answer, award two points to the person who chose the word. Be sure to choose words that no one will know. You can also simply play the boxed version of this game, which is called Balderdash.

After you've played a number of rounds, ask:
- **What was the purpose of this game?** (To find out what these words meant; to fool people with our definitions.)
- **What did you discover about the words we used in this game?** (They have surprising meanings; I didn't know what they meant.)
- **If we put your name on a sheet of paper and asked you to write a definition, what would you write?** (Answers will vary.)

Age Adjustments

YOUNGER CHILDREN **may not be able to play the fictionary game without an adult's help. Very young children may wish to play a simple "name identification" game instead. To do this, set objects or pictures of objects on a table and have children name those objects. Then begin calling objects by the wrong names and ask children why that's wrong. Help them see that using a name in the right way is what God is talking about in the third commandment.**

Have a volunteer read aloud the following names of God from the Bible:
- God the Father
- God over all the kingdoms of the earth
- God my Savior
- God who gives endurance and encouragement
- The Great King above all Kings
- The God who sees me
- Alpha and Omega
- Holy and righteous One
- Counselor
- Spirit of faith
- Teacher
- The Good Shepherd

 Invite family members to share other names for God. Then **read** aloud Exodus 20:7 and Matthew 5:34. Ask:
- **What do these Bible passages tell us about the importance of names?** (God's name is something to respect; we shouldn't misuse words or names.)

Share: We learned in our game that words have meanings—and that sometimes those meanings can surprise us. God's name has a significant meaning and He wants us to treat His name respectfully.

ACTIVITY 2: Toss Carefully

Point: We need to treat His name with respect for it represents God who is holy.

 Supplies: You'll need eggs, a checkbook, and a Bible.

Activity: Take your family outdoors and enjoy an "egg toss" activity. Have family members take turns carefully tossing a raw egg to one another. Have fun with this and encourage family members to toss the egg as far as possible without breaking it. You may prefer to use a water balloon if the weather permits.

 After playing for a while, ask:

- **What was special about the way you had to play this game?** (We had to toss the egg carefully; we had to be gentle with the egg.)
- **What would happen (or did happen) if you were careless with the egg?** (It would break; it would make a mess.)

Write each of your children a check and sign it in front of them. You may need to explain to younger children that a check can be turned in for "real money" at a bank. If possible, choose to write checks that you really want to give to your children. You could do this as a creative allowance activity, or simply offer a "bonus" to your children at this time.

 Then ask:

- **What would be a wrong way to treat the check I just gave you?** (Writing on it; tearing it; losing it.)

Share: Just as we handled the egg with respect, and as we'll handle the checks with respect, we should handle God's name with respect. When we are foolish and use God's name in bad ways, it's kind of like tossing an egg carelessly or tearing up a valuable check. It shows disrespect for

Age Adjustments

OLDER CHILDREN AND TEENAGERS face lots of temptation to use inappropriate language. Peer pressure can be quite strong when it comes to language of today's youth. Talk with your children about their friends' use of language and help them to understand that it shows great wisdom and strength of character when you choose not to use God's name in vain.

God when we use His name in a wrong way.

 Read aloud Psalm 99:3.

Share: When we use God's name, let's use it in a respectful manner, such as to praise Him or to talk to Him in prayer.

WRAP-UP

Gather everyone in a circle and have family members take turns answering this question: **What's one thing you've learned about God today?**

Next, tell kids you've got a new "Life Slogan" you'd like to share with them.

Life Slogan: Today's Life Slogan is this: "You shall not misuse the name of the Lord your God." Have family members repeat the slogan two or three times to help them learn it. Then encourage them to practice saying it during the week so they can talk about it at your next family night session.

Close in Prayer: Allow time for each family member to share prayer concerns and answers to prayer. Then close your time together with prayer for each concern. Thank God for listening to and caring about us.

Remember to record your prayer requests so you can refer to them in the future as you see God answering them.

ⓔ 6: Commandment Four
Remember the Sabbath Day by keeping it holy

Teaching children that the Sabbath has two purposes: rest and reflection on what God has done for us

Scripture
- Genesis 2:2-3
- Exodus 20:8-11; 31:12-17
- Mark 2:27-28
- Hebrews 12:1-4

ACTIVITY OVERVIEW		
Activity	Summary	Pre-Session Prep
Activity 1: In the Air	Keep a bunch of balloons in the air and learn the value of giving God the Sabbath as a day of rest.	You'll need a Bible, balloons, markers, 1 small stone per child, paper, and pencil(s).
Activity 2: Focus	Attempt to recite a memorized poem while being interrupted.	You'll need a Bible, poster board, crayons and/or black and red markers, a $5 bill, and tape.

Main Points:

—A time of rest helps us to refocus on God and brings purpose to all our weekly activity—to serve Him.

—By setting aside the time to focus on God, we have a chance to reflect on His glory and goodness in our "busy" lives.

LIFE SLOGAN: "Remember the Sabbath Day by keeping it holy."

Make it your own
In the space provided below, outline the flow and add any additional ideas to guide you through the process of conducting this family night.

Prayer & Praise Items
In the space provided below, list any items you wish to pray about or give praise for during this family night session.

Journal
In the space provided below, capture a record of any fun or meaningful things which happened during this family night session.

Session Tip

We intentionally have provided more material than we would expect to be used in a single "Family Night" session. You know your family's unique interests and life circumstances best, so feel free to adapt this lesson to meet your family members' needs. Remember, short and simple is better than long and comprehensive.

WARM-UP

Open with Prayer: Begin by having a family member pray, asking God to help everyone in the family understand more about Him through this time. After prayer, review your last lesson by asking these questions:

- **What did we learn about in our last lesson?**
- **What was the Life Slogan?**
- **Have your actions changed because of what we learned? If so, how?** Encourage family members to give specific examples of how they've applied learning from the past week.

Share: Today we're going to study the fourth commandment: Remember the Sabbath Day by keeping it holy.

ACTIVITY 1: In the Air

Point: A time of rest helps us to refocus on God and brings purpose to all our weekly activity—to serve Him.

Supplies: You'll need a Bible, balloons, markers, 1 small stone per child, paper, and pencil(s).

Activity: Busy, busy, busy . . . this seems to be the modern-day mantra that exits from the mouths of literally everyone in this day and age. This activity will give you a forum for family discussion on the role of "rest" and "reflection" in our too-busy lives.

Have each member of your family create a list of his or her responsibilities during a typical week. You'll want to help make the lists for younger children.

When the lists are complete, help family members place each responsibility in a larger category such as school, social, church, family, chores, and so on.

(Your family members may or may not mention faith-related things such as "reading the Bible" or "praying" because these things may take only a small amount of time during the day. Help them to see that God is really a big part of their day and should have a category of His own.)

When the larger categories have been determined, give family members each three or more balloons and have them do the following:

1—Prioritize their lists to see which category takes up the most of their day or week.

2—Place a small stone in one of the balloons, then blow up the balloon and mark on it the thing they spend the most time on. For example, if the top item in their priority list is school, have them write "school" on the balloon.

3—Have family members blow up the rest of their balloons and label them according to the next few items on their priority list.

4—One at a time, have family members toss all the balloons in the air and try to keep them from touching the ground. (Younger children might simply toss three balloons—but make sure one of them is the "God" or "Faith" balloon.)

After allowing each family member a chance to keep the balloons in the air, ask:

- **Was it easy to focus in on one balloon when you had to keep so many airborne?** (No, I kept dropping one; it was hard to keep them in the air.)
- **How did you have to deal with the top priority balloon (the one with the pebble)?** (I had to spend most of my time keeping it in the air; it kept falling faster than the others.)

Now have family members keep their "God" balloons in the air for 2 minutes.

Age Adjustments

YOUNGER CHILDREN won't have much of a concept of priorities, but they will understand the need to rest. To help them see the value of resting, give small children an active thing to do (such as running around the yard). After they've done this for a while, have them pause. Give your child a drink of cold water and talk about how they feel and why it's important to rest. Then make the connection that God wants us to rest from our busy days too. And just as a drink of cold water helps us to rest and grow strong for the next day, spending time with God on our day of rest helps us grow stronger on the inside to face the coming week.

 Then ask:
- **How easy is it to keep one in the air and why?** (It was easy since there was just one balloon; it was much easier than trying to keep lots in the air.)

 Read Genesis 2:2-3; Exodus 20:8-11; and 31:12-17. Then consider the following questions:
- **Why is God so serious in telling us that He wants us to "rest"?** (We are His people and we are to do as God has done; He rested on the seventh day of Creation.)

Share: By observing the Sabbath and "resting" from the many busy things we do, we set ourselves apart and show God we choose to serve Him. Also, when we take time out to rest and think about our relationship with God, other people see that we serve God. They learn that we value our church day and want to keep it holy, as the Bible asks us to do.

ACTIVITY 2: Focus

Point: By setting aside the time to focus on God, we have a chance to reflect on His glory and goodness in our "busy" lives.

 Supplies: You'll need a Bible, poster board, crayons and/or black and red markers, a $5 bill, and tape.

Activity: Read Mark 2:27-28 and Hebrews 12:1-3. Have family members help you draw a "target" on poster board big enough for all to clearly see. Ask children to apply the finishing touches by coloring the center (bull's-eye) of the target red.

Explain the purpose of a target and why the bull's-eye is the most important part of the target. **Share: Whenever archers or marksmen aim at a target, they always aim at the bull's-eye. Those who practice their trade are able to hit the bull's-eye more often than those who don't.**

Place the target on a wall in your meeting area. Make sure it is in plain view. Next, take a monetary note of significant value, such as a $5 bill, and secure it in the center of the bull's-eye. Explain to your children that if they are able to "focus" on the upcoming activity, the $5 bill is theirs.

Have each child, one by one, stand and recite something they have memorized. (This could be the Lord's Prayer, the Pledge of Allegiance, a favorite poem, or anything similar that has more than a

few lines in it.) After they've practiced their speech a couple times, ask if they know it well enough to "compete" for the bull's-eye reward.

To win the money, your child must be able to recite their speech word for word five times in a row, pausing in the middle of a speech whenever you ask a question. When you ask a question, your child must answer the question, then pick up exactly where he or she left off in the recitation of the memorized speech.

As facilitator, you are now ready to test your child's ability to keep "focused." As a child begins, politely interrupt him or her as often as you want and ask "off the wall" questions, such as: "What time is it in Belfast, Ireland ?" "What was Hank Aaron's lifetime batting average?" and "What is the prettiest color in the rainbow?" Choose silly questions that will distract children from the task at hand and ask as many as you need to trip them up and cause them to miss their place in the memorized speech.

 If someone wins the money, celebrate their ability to focus when distracted. Then ask:

- **Why could you recite your memorization initially?** (I had no distractions.)
- **What was difficult about reciting the memorized speech when I kept asking you questions?** (I could not focus; it was hard to concentrate.)

Share: It is important to spend a regular time focusing on God. We do this when we pray, and when we take time out to follow the fourth commandment each week and "keep the Sabbath holy."

 Read Hebrews 12:1-4 and Mark 2:27-28. Then **share: When we focus on God, we come closer to hitting the bull's-eye in our relationship with God. When we take time out each week and spend time at church, in prayer, and learning more about God, we grow closer to Him.**

 Ask:

- **How can we as a family "keep the Sabbath Day holy"?** (Attend church together; have a family meal time; spend time together on Sunday.)

Share: God rested on the seventh day when He created the world, and He wants us to rest too. Let us make plans to give God our full attention each week and keep our church day holy.

WRAP-UP

Gather everyone in a circle and have family members take turns answering this question: **What's one thing you've learned about God today?**

Next, tell kids you've got a new "Life Slogan" you'd like to share with them.

Life Slogan: Today's Life Slogan is this: "Remember the Sabbath Day by keeping it holy." Have family members repeat the slogan two or three times to help them learn it. Then encourage them to practice saying it during the week so they can talk about it at your next family night session.

Close in Prayer: Allow time for each family member to share prayer concerns and answers to prayer. Then close your time together with prayer for each concern. Thank God for listening to and caring about us.

Remember to record your prayer requests so you can refer to them in the future as you see God answering them.

7: Commandment Five
You shall honor your father and mother

Teaching children the importance of honoring their parents

Scripture
- Luke 15:11-32
- Exodus 20:12
- Deuteronomy 5:16

ACTIVITY OVERVIEW		
Activity	Summary	Pre-Session Prep
Activity 1: Balloon Wars	List things that honor and dishonor parents and compete in a fun contest.	You'll need a balloon, two pieces of different colored paper, and pencils.
Activity 2: Stories of Honor	Share stories of children who honored their parents and talk about the rewards of honoring parents.	You'll need Bibles.

Main Points:
— Honoring your parents teaches you to honor God.
— God commands us to honor because it is good for us.

LIFE SLOGAN: "You shall honor your father and mother."

Make it your own
In the space provided below, outline the flow and add any additional ideas to guide you through the process of conducting this family night.

Prayer & Praise Items
In the space provided below, list any items you wish to pray about or give praise for during this family night session.

Journal
In the space provided below, capture a record of any fun or meaningful things which happened during this family night session.

WARM-UP

Open with Prayer: Begin by having a family member pray, asking God to help everyone in the family understand more about Him through this time. After prayer, review your last lesson by asking these questions:

- **What did we learn about in our last lesson?**
- **What was the Life Slogan?**
- **Have your actions changed because of what we learned? If so, how?** Encourage family members to give specific examples of how they've applied learning from the past week.

Share: Today we're going to learn about the fifth commandment which tells us to honor our parents.

ACTIVITY 1: Balloon Wars

Point: Honoring your parents teaches you to honor God.

 Supplies: You'll need a balloon, colored paper, and pencils.

Activity: Take a few minutes to explain the concept of "honoring" to your children. Have them copy the following examples of what it means to honor parents each on a separate sheet of paper:

- Doing what has been asked the first time
- Saying you love me without being asked
- Doing a job before being asked
- Responding right away when questioned
- Telling the truth even when it may get you in trouble
- Speaking in kind, warm tones instead of yelling

Have the children come up with a few of their own "what it means to honor" phrases and list these on individual, large pieces of paper. Then, on different colored and very small pieces of paper, have them list phrases they think reflect dishonor to mom and dad. For example, kids might list:

- Lying
- Not obeying right away
- Shouting instead of talking calmly
- Breaking house rules

Have children crumple up each sheet of paper into a ball, keeping the two categories (large and small paper wads) separate. Divide into two teams and give the large paper wads (honor phrases) to one team and the small paper wads (dishonor) to the other.

Blow up a balloon and place it in the middle of the room. Have the two teams stand on opposite sides of the room, facing the balloon. Explain that the object of the game is to knock the balloon to the opposing team's side by tossing the paper wads at the balloon. Play this game for a while and enjoy the controlled mayhem. Allow participants to pick up their own paper wads and toss them again and again until they successfully get the balloon to the other side of the room. (After one successful round, switch sides and paper wad piles to give each side a chance to experience victory.)

Age Adjustments

Since YOUNGER CHILDREN may not be able to read, you can simplify this activity by using different colored papers for the honoring and dishonoring statements. Or you can mark with a smiley face, those that honor parents and with a frown face, those that dishonor parents. This will allow younger, nonreading children to participate in a fun way.

 After the game, collect the papers in a big pile and discuss the following questions:

- **Was it easier to win using the large "honor" paper wads or the small "dishonor" paper wads?** (The "honor" wads. It is hard to win when you have only small paper wads.)
- **How is this like the fifth commandment?** (Life goes better when we honor rather than dishonor our parents.)

Share: When we choose to honor our parents, God says we "win" in life—just like winning in the balloon paper wad game.

ACTIVITY 2: Stories of Honor

Point: God commands "honoring" for our benefit.

 Supplies: You'll need Bibles.

Activity: Have children tell you stories of people they know from literature (or popular media) who disobeyed their parents (Pinnochio, Kevin in *Home Alone,* etc.). Share your own stories of

people who honored their parents and those who didn't—and the consequences of both kinds of behavior. You might want to summarize the story of the prodigal son, from Luke 15:11-32, as an example of one son who chose to dishonor his family.

 Help children scour the daily newspapers to find articles about good and bad events in your community and around the world. For each article, consider discussing the following questions:

- **Do you think this person honored his or her parents? Why or why not?**
- **How does the way we treat parents affect our choices as we grow up?**

Review Exodus 20:12 and Deuteronomy 5:16. Discuss how honoring parents can help children make good decisions in life.

Then ask:
- **If a child wants to honor his or her parents, what kinds of choices should he or she make?** (Good choices; things that will make parents proud.)

Share: When we honor our parents, we take time to think about the things we do. God wants us to honor our parents because it helps us to make good choices in life—and because our parents deserve respect and love. God too wants us to honor Him and make choices that will make Him proud.

Age Adjustments

OLDER CHILDREN AND TEENAGERS **might benefit from a more powerful example of what it looks like to dishonor parents. Consider taking older children on a tour of a local juvenile hall or jail. Afterward, discuss how behaviors that dishonor parents and dishonor God can lead to consequences such as jail time and trouble with the law. Explain that, while some of the people who do wrong things didn't have loving parents who they could honor, others could have avoided dire situations just by thinking about how their actions would honor or dishonor their parents. Make sure kids know that they're ultimately responsible for their own actions, but that the addition of "filters" that ask, "Does this honor my parents?" and, "Does this honor God?" can help them make good decisions.**

WRAP-UP

Gather everyone in a circle and have family members take turns answering this question: **What's one thing you've learned about God today?**

Next, tell kids you've got a new "Life Slogan" you'd like to share with them.

Life Slogan: Today's Life Slogan is this: "You shall honor your father and mother." Have family members repeat the slogan two or three times to help them learn it. Then encourage them to practice saying it during the week so they can talk about it at your next family night session.

 **Close in Prayer:** Allow time for each family member to share prayer concerns and answers to prayer. Then close your time together with prayer for each concern. Thank God for listening to and caring about us.

Remember to record your prayer requests so you can refer to them in the future as you see God answering them.

⊚ 8: Commandment Six
You shall not murder

Teaching children the value and sanctity of life

Scripture
- Exodus 20:13
- Matthew 22:37-39
- Genesis 4:8-10
- Matthew 5:23-26
- Matthew 6:9-13

ACTIVITY OVERVIEW		
Activity	Summary	Pre-Session Prep
Activity 1: Intent	Pitch pennies and discover what it means to "intend harm" to someone and why it's wrong.	You'll need pennies and a Bible.
Activity 2: Letting Go	Learn how to let go of something to gain something else; then compare that to forgiveness.	You'll need basketballs (or other large balls), a bowl of M&Ms®, and a Bible.

Main Points:
—Murder, and the attitude that causes people to murder, is sinful.

—We need to solve our differences and forgive before our attitude or actions become wrongful.

LIFE SLOGAN: "You shall not murder."

Make it your own
In the space provided below, outline the flow and add any additional ideas to guide you through the process of conducting this family night.

Prayer & Praise Items
In the space provided below, list any items you wish to pray about or give praise for during this family night session.

Journal
In the space provided below, capture a record of any fun or meaningful things which happened during this family night session.

Session Tip

We intentionally have provided more material than we would expect to be used in a single "Family Night" session. You know your family's unique interests and life circumstances best, so feel free to adapt this lesson to meet your family members' needs. Remember, short and simple is better than long and comprehensive.

 WARM-UP

Open with Prayer: Begin by having a family member pray, asking God to help everyone in the family understand more about Him through this time. After prayer, review your last lesson by asking these questions:

• **What did we learn about in our last lesson?**
• **What was the Life Slogan?**
• **Have your actions changed because of what we learned? If so, how?** Encourage family members to give specific examples of how they've applied learning from the past week.

Share: Today we're going to learn about the value and meaning of God's sixth commandment, which is "You shall not murder."

ACTIVITY 1: Intent

Point: Murder, and the attitude that causes people to murder, is sinful.

Supplies: You'll need pennies and a Bible.

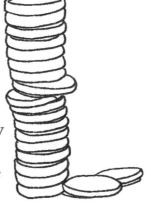

Activity: Give each family member a supply of pennies. Choose an area in your house (or outside) where you can "pitch pennies" against a wall. Explain the object of the game: to get your penny closest to the place where the wall meets the floor. Have family members take turns tossing one penny and determine which toss is closest to the wall. Award one point each round to the person with the best penny toss.

Afterward, explain the meaning of the word *intent* and ask:
• **What was your purpose or intent when playing this game?** (To win; to beat the other guy; to get my penny closer to the wall; to score the most points.)

• **What are other things in life you do "on purpose" or with intent?** (I wash my face on purpose; I choose what I want for a snack; I tickle my brother.)

Share: We do lots of things on purpose or with intent. But sometimes, people do bad things on purpose. One of these is warned against in the sixth commandment: do not murder anyone. (See Exodus 20:13.)

 Ask:
• **What does murder mean?** (Answer: To kill intentionally or on purpose.)
• **Why is it wrong to intentionally hurt or kill someone?** (People are valuable to God; God wants people to be nice to each other.)
• **What are the two greatest commands?** (Read Matthew 22:37-39 and summarize these if necessary.)

Share: God wants us to love one another. People who murder and kill others on purpose don't show love, they show hate. Love is the opposite of hate and anger. Love for God and love for your neighbor cannot exist with hate and anger in your heart at the same time.

 Read Genesis 4:8-10 and explain that this was the first murder. Then ask:
• **Why did Cain want to kill Abel?** (Cain was jealous of Abel; Cain didn't like Abel.)

Share: The first murder shows us how sometimes people do bad things because they are selfish. Murder, and the desire to hurt people, comes from being selfish and thinking only of ourselves.

Take a few minutes to talk with your children about the feelings they've had when they wanted a toy someone else had; or about the feelings they had when someone did something wrong to them. Explain that it's okay to be upset, and okay to be angry or want something, but that it's always wrong to hurt people in order to get our way. You may even be able to refer to headlines in your local paper that can shed light on the sadness God must feel when people murder.

Age Adjustments

OLDER CHILDREN AND TEENAGERS are dealing with strong feelings as they grow toward adulthood. Use this activity to help them see that dealing with anger and hate appropriately is the only way to resolve conflicts. Your children may read in the newspaper about teens who explode in anger and hurt or murder others. Take time to talk about why some people choose the path of death and destruction. Then spend time in prayer together, asking God to lead your family members to make good decisions in life that honor the sanctity of life and to comfort those who have been affected by the careless and sinful act of murder.

ACTIVITY 2: Letting Go

Point: We need to try to solve our differences and forgive before our attitude or actions become wrongful.

 Supplies: You'll need basketballs (or other large balls), a bowl of M&Ms®, and a Bible.

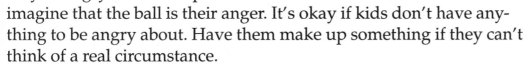

Activity: Have family members participate in this activity one at a time. Bring one person in the room and have him or her sit and hold out their hands, palms up. Place a ball in each upturned hand. Next label each ball—one "anger" and one "hate." Ask the family members to think of something that they're angry at another person about and imagine that the ball is their anger. It's okay if kids don't have anything to be angry about. Have them make up something if they can't think of a real circumstance.

Then hold out a bowl of M&Ms® (or other similar candies) and offer some to the family member. When he or she puts down the ball to collect the candy, call in the next family member and repeat the activity.

 After each person has done this activity, consider the following question:
- **What did you have to do to get the candy?** (I had to put down the ball; I couldn't get it because the ball was in my hand.)

 Read Matthew 5:23-26, then ask:
- **How is putting down the ball to get the candy like forgiving someone?** (You cannot love and hate someone at the same time; we have to fix the problem before things are good; you can't hang on to the anger forever.)

Recite the Lord's Prayer together (see Matthew 6:9-13).

 Ask:
- **What does this prayer tell us about forgiveness?** (We're supposed to forgive one another; we should forgive others just as God has forgiven us.)

Share: If we hold onto anger or bad attitudes, we are heading for trouble. God wants us to deal with those problems and forgive others so we can enjoy a healthy relationship with them, just as we were able to enjoy candy when we put down the basketball.

WRAP-UP

Gather everyone in a circle and have family members take turns answering this question: **What's one thing you've learned about God today?**

Next, tell kids you've got a new "Life Slogan" you'd like to share with them.

Life Slogan: Today's Life Slogan is this: "You shall not murder." Have family members repeat the slogan two or three times to help them learn it. Then encourage them to practice saying it during the week so they can talk about it at your next family night session.

Close in Prayer: Allow time for each family member to share prayer concerns and answers to prayer. Then close your time together with prayer for each concern. Thank God for listening to and caring about us.

Remember to record your prayer requests so you can refer to them in the future as you see God answering them.

9: Commandment Seven
You shall not commit adultery

Teaching children the importance of the gift of sex in marriage

Scripture
- 1 Thessalonians 4:3-8
- Exodus 20:14
- Matthew 5:27-28
- Psalm 119:9

ACTIVITY OVERVIEW		
Activity	Summary	Pre-Session Prep
Activity 1: Special Gift	Learn about the "special-ness" of the gift of sexuality.	You'll need your child's favorite candy beautifully wrapped, masking tape, and a Bible.
Activity 2: God Sees Everything	Play a game and learn how God knows our hearts.	You'll need three large moving boxes and a Bible.

Main Points:
- —Sex was given to adults as a gift to be enjoyed only in marriage, as a sign of commitment and trust.
- —Intent to commit sexual sin is as wrong as the act itself.

LIFE SLOGAN: "You shall not commit adultery."

Make it your own

In the space provided below, outline the flow and add any additional ideas to guide you through the process of conducting this family night.

Prayer & Praise Items

In the space provided below, list any items you wish to pray about or give praise for during this family night session.

Journal

In the space provided below, capture a record of any fun or meaningful things which happened during this family night session.

We intentionally have provided more material than we would expect to be used in a single "Family Night" session. You know your family's unique interests and life circumstances best, so feel free to adapt this lesson to meet your family members' needs. Remember, short and simple is better than long and comprehensive.

WARM-UP

Open with Prayer: Begin by having a family member pray, asking God to help everyone in the family understand more about Him through this time. After prayer, review your last lesson by asking these questions:

- **What did we learn about in our last lesson?**
- **What was the Life Slogan?**
- **Have your actions changed because of what we learned? If so, how?** Encourage family members to give specific examples of how they've applied learning from the past week.

Share: Today we will learn about the seventh commandment: You shall not commit adultery.

ACTIVITY 1: Special Gift

Point: Sex was given to adults as a gift to be enjoyed only in marriage, as a sign of commitment and trust.

 Supplies: You'll need your child's favorite candy beautifully wrapped, masking tape, and a Bible.

Activity: Choose a favorite candy or toy to give to each family member and wrap each in wrapping paper decorated with ribbons and bows. Make the packages as pretty as you can. Write the name of the gift recipient on each package. When everyone is in the room, give a wrong gift to each family member and have him or her open it. When the gifts are all opened, say something like, "oops, these were given to the wrong per-

Age Adjustments

YOUNGER CHILDREN may not be ready for a lesson discussing sexuality. You know your children and their ability to understand. Make wise decisions about who you will include in this family activity. If you have especially young children, save this lesson for later (when they're older). If your young children have already been exposed to the negative aspects of sexuality, this may be an appropriate lesson. But only teach this lesson if you are prepared to answer their inevitable questions (which may be many). Use good judgment on when it's right to share this topic with your children.

son," then hand out masking tape so family members can quickly rewrap the gifts and give them to their rightful recipients. Once again, have family members open their gifts.

 Consider these questions:
• **How did it feel to receive a present that was already opened?** (It wasn't as much fun; it didn't seem special; I already knew what was in it.)

Share: Television, movies, and music teach us that sex is something that is fun—and that is okay for people to enjoy even if they're not married. Well, they got it half right: sex is fun. God thought it up in the first place, but it was intended only for people who have made the commitment of a lifetime together through marriage. Sex is a gift from God to adults that is meant for marriage only, not before marriage or outside of marriage. When people choose to "open the gift of sexuality" before marriage, they take away the specialness of that gift from their husband or wife.

God commands us to be pure. Let's see what He says about waiting until marriage to enjoy the gift of sexuality.

 Read 1 Thessalonians 4:3-8 and Exodus 20:14, then ask:
• **Why do you think God made this a commandment?**
(To protect us; to show the importance of marriage.)

Summarize the following possible reasons God chose to make this a commandment:
• Sex outside of marriage takes advantage of a person physically without any trust or commitment to the relationship.
• Someone always gets hurt when sex is taken out of a marriage context.
• People feel guilty.
• There is a risk of unwanted pregnancy.
• People could get sexually transmitted diseases.
• Purity protects the "specialness" of the gift of marriage.
• Disobeying God is wrong. God tells us not enter into immorality.
• Sex outside of marriage violates the "temple of God"—our bodies.
• Sex objectifies people—makes them "objects" rather than individuals.

Say: A husband and wife come together as one in more than just the

physical way when they enjoy the gift of sex; there is a spiritual element as well. The excitement of "discovering/opening" the gift together is something God wants for all people who someday marry.

If you have teenagers in your family, consider taking time for a prayer asking God for strength and wisdom as they begin to relate to members of the opposite sex. Ask God to protect your children from the temptation to open the gift of sex before marriage.

ACTIVITY 2: God Sees Everything

Point: Intent to commit sexual sin is as wrong as the act itself.

 Supplies: You'll need three large moving boxes and a Bible.

Activity: Place three large boxes (big enough for you or your children to fit in) on their sides with the openings facing the same direction. (If you can't find three large boxes, you can set up three card tables or other pieces of furniture and cover them with sheets.)

Stand behind the boxes and send all family members except for one child into another room. Have the child hide in one of the boxes as you look on. Then invite the rest of the family back into the room. Have family members guess which box the child is in. Award a point for each correct guess and repeat the game as many times as you like. Each time, be sure you know where the family member is hiding as this is important to the discussion of this activity.

 Consider these questions:
* **How was the way a family member hid in a box like the way we sometimes try to hide things we did that are wrong?** (We can hide them sometimes; we can't always hide.)
* **How was the role I played like the role God plays in our lives?** (God sees everything; God knows when we try to hide things.)

 Read Matthew 5:27-28 and then ask:
* **How does God tell us we can overcome the temptation to sin?** (We must use self-control; we need to control our thoughts and actions.)

69

Read Psalm 119:9. Then **share: There are lots of things we can do to protect ourselves from the sin of sexual impurity. The Bible tells us that the secret thoughts we have of wanting to sin are just as bad as acting on those thoughts. So what can we do? Here are a few ideas:**

You may have heard the phrase: Garbage in, garbage out. This means that if we focus on things that are impure or negative, we'll begin to act that way too. But when we focus on what is good, pure, and righteous, we will live a good, pure, and righteous life.

God wants us to guard our minds too and be careful what we watch, look at, and think about. We must also consider the consequences of our actions and think about the future. It's easy to think about the good feelings we might have in the short term and forget about the long-term consequences. We must learn to develop personal boundaries that we simply will not cross. We must pray for the purity of ourselves and our future spouses. We must avoid relationships that are unequally yoked—in other words, don't choose to date someone who isn't a Christian.

Have family members comment on the following statements:
- **Sin is contagious. Our sin nature pulls us away from righteous living. It looks attractive to us.**
- **We shouldn't be in a romantic relationship with a nonbeliever because he or she lives in this world and we are called to not be of this world. What is important to us is not important to the nonbeliever.**

Share: When we enter a relationship that may grow into romantic love, we must respect the other person and not fall into sin. God will help to protect us from thinking impure thoughts if we ask Him for strength. And He can help us stay pure until marriage, where two people can finally unwrap one of the most exciting gifts God offers His people.

WRAP-UP

Gather everyone in a circle and have family members take turns answering this question: **What's one thing you've learned about God today?**

Next, tell kids you've got a new "Life Slogan" you'd like to share with them.

Life Slogan: Today's Life Slogan is this: "You shall not commit adultery."
Have family members repeat the slogan two or three times to help

them learn it. Then encourage them to practice saying it during the week so they can talk about it at your next family night session.

Close in Prayer: Allow time for each family member to share prayer concerns and answers to prayer. Then close your time together with prayer for each concern. Thank God for listening to and caring about us.

Remember to record your prayer requests so you can refer to them in the future as you see God answering them.

10: Commandment Eight
You shall not steal

Teaching children that stealing is against God's will, is wrong, and it is a sin

Scripture
- Exodus 20:15
- Joshua 6:12-27; 7:1-26

ACTIVITY OVERVIEW		
Activity	Summary	Pre-Session Prep
Activity 1: Stealing Memories	Experience what it might be like to have something "stolen" and define stealing.	You'll need valuable family items, such as old coins, Grandpa's old pocket watch, the "handed down" generational family Bible, and so on.
Activity 2: Caught!	Play a game where they try to get away with something and discuss the consequences of stealing.	You'll need a bandana and a Bible.

Main Points:
— We need to respect others' property.
— You can choose to obey or not obey, but you can't choose the consequences.

LIFE SLOGAN: "You shall not steal."

Make it your own
In the space provided below, outline the flow and add any additional ideas to guide you through the process of conducting this family night.

Prayer & Praise Items
In the space provided below, list any items you wish to pray about or give praise for during this family night session.

Journal
In the space provided below, capture a record of any fun or meaningful things which happened during this family night session.

Session Tip

We intentionally have provided more material than we would expect to be used in a single "Family Night" session. You know your family's unique interests and life circumstances best, so feel free to adapt this lesson to meet your family members' needs. Remember, short and simple is better than long and comprehensive.

WARM-UP

Open with Prayer: Begin by having a family member pray, asking God to help everyone in the family understand more about Him through this time. After prayer, review your last lesson by asking these questions:

- **What did we learn about in our last lesson?**
- **What was the Life Slogan?**
- **Have your actions changed because of what we learned? If so, how?** Encourage family members to give specific examples of how they've applied learning from the past week.

Share: Today we're going to learn about the eighth commandment: You shall not steal.

ACTIVITY 1: Stealing Memories

Point: We need to respect others' property.

Supplies: You'll need valuable family items, such as old coins, Grandpa's old pocket watch, the "handed down" generational family Bible, and so on.

Activity: Ahead of time, sneak up into your children's rooms and "steal" their most prized possessions. Hide the valuable family items you selected somewhere in your meeting room, out of sight.

Read aloud Exodus 20:15. Then have each family member give his or her own definition of "stealing." Explain that the Bible has lots of stories about thieves, including the description of the two thieves who were crucified on the crosses on either side of Jesus. Spend up to three minutes talking about stealing. Then ask family members to locate the specific prized possessions and bring them to your meeting room. Allow a few moments for searching, then call everyone together and discuss the following:

- **What was it like to try and find [your possession] and discover that it is missing?** (I was worried; it made me feel sad.)
- **Let me reassure you that the items aren't stolen. But why would you miss these items if they were?** (Because it means a lot to me; because it brings me comfort; because it reminds me of good things.)

Share: Even though the possessions you were looking for were just "things," they each had a special meaning for you. Many of our possessions have value that can't be counted in dollars. When someone steals something of value from us, that item can't always be replaced.

 Ask:

- **What concern does a thief have for another person's property?** (None; a thief only thinks of himself.)
- **What does it mean to respect each other's property?** (Let people keep their own stuff; don't take or break things that belong to others.)

Return the possessions to your family members.

ACTIVITY 2: Caught!

Point: You can choose to obey or not obey, but you can't choose the consequences.

Supplies: You'll need a bandana and a Bible.

Activity: Choose a large room or an outdoor location for this activity. You'll be playing "steal the bacon" with your family. Have everyone sit in a large circle surrounding the bandana. Explain the object of the game to your family:

Age Adjustments

OLDER CHILDREN AND TEENAGERS face the temptation and pressure to steal or cheat (which is really just a variation on stealing) because of peer pressure. Talk with them about the pressures they feel and help them see that they can overcome the temptation to steal and make good choices. Encourage them to stand strong in their faith and not ignore the eighth commandment just because friends think it's "no big deal."

to be the person who grabs the bandana and returns to his or her seat before being tagged by another person. Call out the names of two family members at a time and say "go" to start a round. The person who grabs the bandana and gets back to his or her seat without being tagged will receive one point. Play a number of rounds until everyone is tired and out of breath. Sit in a closer circle and continue the lesson.

 Ask:
- **What was the object of this game?** (Steal the bandana; to not get caught.)
- **What did it feel like when you got caught?** (I was disappointed; I felt bad.)

Share: Prisons today are full of people who tried to steal something and got caught. Unlike this game, the consequences of getting caught were quite severe.

For every sin, there is a punishment or a price to pay. In our game, if you got caught you lost the game. However, in real life, that's not the case.

Let's talk about how we should respond to stealing.

 Read Joshua 6:12-27; 7:1-26. Then discuss how someone should respond when he or she has sinned and stolen something:
- **Acknowledge you sinned against God and specifically state your sin.**
- **Ask for God's forgiveness.**
- **Acknowledge your sin to the owner of the item or items, return or compensate for them, and ask for forgiveness.**
- **Face the consequences.**

Take a few moments to talk with your children about your experiences with stealing. This could be simply a temptation you once felt when you were younger; a story of a time when your house was burglarized; or any other example from your life or the lives of those around you.

Allow a time for children to confess their sins (silently or aloud) and ask for forgiveness if they've ever stolen anything. Don't turn this into a big spectacle by berating children or telling them how bad they were for making such a choice. Instead, use this as a time to show how God's forgiveness can help us when we mess up. You may want to help your children come up with a plan for resolving the situation if they've stolen.

Share: When people steal things, they usually think it's no big deal if they never get caught. But when we steal, God always knows and so do we, that we've done something wrong. Let us pray that we will always avoid the temptation to steal and instead, make good choices about how we treat other people's property.

WRAP-UP

Gather everyone in a circle and have family members take turns answering this question: **What's one thing you've learned about God today?**

Next, tell kids you've got a new "Life Slogan" you'd like to share with them.

Life Slogan: Today's Life Slogan is this: **"You shall not steal."** Have family members repeat the slogan two or three times to help them learn it. Then encourage them to practice saying it during the week so they can talk about it at your next family night session.

Close in Prayer: Allow time for each family member to share prayer concerns and answers to prayer. Then close your time together with prayer for each concern. Thank God for listening to and caring about us.

Remember to record your prayer requests so you can refer to them in the future as you see God answering them.

@ 11: Commandment Nine
You shall not lie

Teaching children the importance of telling the truth

Scripture
- Exodus 20:16
- Matthew 5:37
- Matthew 12:36-37

ACTIVITY OVERVIEW		
Activity	Summary	Pre-Session Prep
Activity 1: Spinning Lies	Play a game and learn the consequences of lying.	You'll need a baseball bat or a stick of the same length, masking tape, and a Bible.
Activity 2: Opposites	Learn about how lying is the opposite of the truth and that God desires us to live in truth.	You'll need two magnets and a Bible.

Main Points:
   —Lying has consequences.
   —Truth is the opposite of lying, and God is Truth.

LIFE SLOGAN: "You shall not lie."

Make it your own

In the space provided below, outline the flow and add any additional ideas to guide you through the process of conducting this family night.

Prayer & Praise Items

In the space provided below, list any items you wish to pray about or give praise for during this family night session.

Journal

In the space provided below, capture a record of any fun or meaningful things which happened during this family night session.

Session Tip

We intentionally have provided more material than we would expect to be used in a single "Family Night" session. You know your family's unique interests and life circumstances best, so feel free to adapt this lesson to meet your family members' needs. Remember, short and simple is better than long and comprehensive.

WARM-UP

Open with Prayer: Begin by having a family member pray, asking God to help everyone in the family understand more about Him through this time. After prayer, review your last lesson by asking these questions:

- **What did we learn about in our last lesson?**
- **What was the Life Slogan?**
- **Have your actions changed because of what we learned? If so, how?** Encourage family members to give specific examples of how they've applied learning from the past week.

Share: Today we're going to learn about the ninth commandment: You shall not lie.

ACTIVITY 1: Spinning Lies

Point: Lying has consequences

 Supplies: You'll need a baseball bat or a stick of the same length, masking tape, and a Bible.

Activity: Tape a straight line about 10 feet down the middle of the floor in a large room that has been cleared of obstacles. Place a baseball bat or a stick of approximately the same length at one end of the line.

Have family members (this means you too!), one at a time: race down the taped line, set the bat on one end, place their hand on the other end, set their head on their hand and spin in place five to ten times. Then have them run down the taped line (in as straight a line as possible) to tag another family member who will repeat the activity.

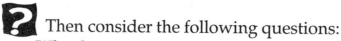

Repeat this game so each person gets at least two turns spinning and attempting to run a straight line.

 Then consider the following questions:
- **What happened when you tried to run down the line after spinning?** (We waved to the right or left; we couldn't walk straight.)

- **What were the consequences of spinning?** (Getting dizzy; going slow; not being able to run straight.)

Share: When we spun around and tried to walk straight, we couldn't do it because of the way the spinning affected our balance. The same is true when people "spin" lies or tell "tall tales." There are consequences to telling lies.

 Read Exodus 20:16 and Matthew 5:37. Then discuss:
- **What does the Bible say about our words?** (We shouldn't go "outside the lines" and tell lies; we should speak the truth.)

Take a few moments to role play a few situations with your children. You'll want to tailor these situations to the ages of your children, but here are a couple to get you started:
- You and your friends are in a restaurant that gives free ice cream on your birthday. You decide to give in to your friends' taunting and lie about your birthday to get free ice cream. Now your parents have found out. What do you say? What are the consequences of your lie?
- You "borrow" the answers to an important test in school and copy them so you can get a good grade when you take the test. Your teacher finds out. What do you say? What are the consequences of your lie?
- You break a valuable lamp while your parents are away, but tell them someone else did it. What do you say when your parents find out you did it? What are the consequences of your lie?

For each of these role plays, have one person play the part of the child and the other play the part of the parent or teacher. Then discuss these situations and how they might have been avoided.

Age Adjustments

OLDER CHILDREN AND TEENAGERS are experts at explaining away lies. Many prefer to see lies in degrees. They believe "little white lies" aren't as bad as "big, bold lies" and therefore often lie to parents or others because they don't see the lies as that dangerous. Talk with your older children about the possible consequences of "little white lies"—they can grow into big lies; they set a bad pattern; people can still be hurt; and God sees all lies as wrong. Make a commitment together to avoid compartmentalizing lies according to perceived severity and, instead, to avoid lying altogether.

ACTIVITY 2: Opposites

Point: Truth is the opposite of lying, and God is Truth.

 Supplies: You'll need two magnets and a Bible.

Activity: Give your children two "naked" magnets (magnets that have a north and south pole—not ones that are embedded into plastic holders). Have them walk around the house and experiment to see what things they can pick up with the magnets. For fun, give them a time limit and see how many items they can find that will stick to the magnets.

Next, demonstrate how the magnets can be attracted to each other, and how they can repel each other when both north or both south poles are facing each other. Have children fight the repelling force and see if they can get the ends to meet squarely.

 Ask:

- **How is the force of the magnets repelling each other like the way people try to explain a lie and make it sound like the truth?** (A lie will never match up with the truth; lies and the truth are opposites.)

Have children list as many opposites as they can. Here are a few they might suggest:

Dark - light
Up - down
Inside - outside
Big - little
Man - woman
Dog - cat
Tall - short
Lie - truth

Share: Lying affects others and can hurt them in many different ways. God wants us, as imitators of Christ, to treat others with love and respect. And He wants us to speak the truth and not lie. When we lie, we are doing the opposite of telling the truth and our lives will not match up with Jesus' life just as the magnets don't line up.

Read Matthew 12:36-37. **Share: God looks at the heart and the words we say are a reflection of what is inside. Our words are an outward sign of an inward attitude. We need to be right before God so we can be right before others. If this is a problem for us, we need to pray that the Holy Spirit will fill us with a desire to always tell the truth.**

WRAP-UP

Gather everyone in a circle and have family members take turns answering this question: **What's one thing you've learned about God today?**

Next, tell kids you've got a new "Life Slogan" you'd like to share with them.

Life Slogan: Today's Life Slogan is this: "You shall not lie." Have family members repeat the slogan two or three times to help them learn it. Then encourage them to practice saying it during the week so they can talk about it at your next family night session.

Close in Prayer: Allow time for each family member to share prayer concerns and answers to prayer. Then close your time together with prayer for each concern. Thank God for listening to and caring about us.

Remember to record your prayer requests so you can refer to them in the future as you see God answering them.

⊚ 12: Commandment Ten
You shall not covet

Teaching children the importance of not always "wanting"

Scripture
• Matthew 6:33

ACTIVITY OVERVIEW		
Activity	Summary	Pre-Session Prep
Activity 1: What Really Matters	Learn that God and people are the only things that last and that material goods are only temporary.	You'll need paper, marker, and a Bible.
Activity 2: Grab What You Can	Learn how "wanting" sometimes gets us in trouble.	You'll need pennies or candy, and a box.

Main Points:

— We should be on guard against "wanting." True happiness is not found in things.

— There are only two things that will last, people (relationships) and God's Word.

LIFE SLOGAN: "You shall not covet."

Make it your own

In the space provided below, outline the flow and add any additional ideas to guide you through the process of conducting this family night.

Prayer & Praise Items

In the space provided below, list any items you wish to pray about or give praise for during this family night session.

Journal

In the space provided below, capture a record of any fun or meaningful things which happened during this family night session.

Session Tip

We intentionally have provided more material than we would expect to be used in a single "Family Night" session. You know your family's unique interests and life circumstances best, so feel free to adapt this lesson to meet your family members' needs. Remember, short and simple is better than long and comprehensive.

WARM-UP

Open with Prayer: Begin by having a family member pray, asking God to help everyone in the family understand more about Him through this time. After prayer, review your last lesson by asking these questions:

- **What did we learn about in our last lesson?**
- **What was the Life Slogan?**
- **Have your actions changed because of what we learned?**
  If so, how? Encourage family members to give specific examples of how they've applied learning from the past week.

Share: Today we are going to learn about the tenth commandment: You shall not covet.

ACTIVITY 1: What Really Matters

Point: There are only two things that will last, people (relationships) and God's Word.

 Supplies: You'll need paper, marker, and a Bible.

Activity: Write each of the following letters on a separate piece of paper and give them to your children: RPWDDOGOOEPSLE. Have your children attempt to unscramble the letters to list two things that will last long after material goods have turned to dust. The answer is: People (and) God's Word. If your children are having difficulty with this, put the letters

in three separate piles—one for each word. After unscrambling these letters, read aloud:

 Read Matthew 6:33, then ask:

- **What does this verse mean to us?** (God will take care of our every need; seek God first; our wants are secondary to our relationship with God.)
- **Knowing that what matters most is people and God's Word, how do you think God would want us to live?** (Love others; focus on the needs of others first; love God above all things.)
- **What are ways we can live this out in our own lives?** (Go out of our way to serve others; live like Christ wants you to so that others notice your love; share the Gospel with as many as we can.)

Share: Our relationship with God goes on forever. Our impact on others' lives can also be eternal. But the things we buy or own will someday be gone. Someday our toys will be rusted away and our house will be nothing but ashes, but the friendships we make will live on and our love for God will bring us to heaven—and into His presence.

Have your children join you in prayer, asking for a mind and heart that doesn't covet things, but desires to grow closer to God and build relationships with other people.

ACTIVITY 2: Grab What You Can

Point: We should be on guard against "wanting" for true happiness is not found in things.

 Supplies: You'll need pennies or candy, and a box.

Activity: Cut a hole in the box just big enough for your child's hand to fit into, but not big enough for his or her hand to slip back out when clenched in a fist. Place the pennies or candies in the box. One by one, have children attempt to grab as many candies or pennies as they can with one hand (and without breaking the box

where you've cut the hole). Children may soon discover that they can't get as many items as they'd like because they can't pull their clenched fist out. Repeat this activity for each family member. Some may want to try more than once. Let them.

 Then discuss the following questions:
- **Was it easy or difficult to pick up lots of candy or pennies? Explain.** (It was easy to pick them up, but hard to get them out of the box; it wasn't easy because my hand didn't fit back through the hole.)
- **What were you feeling as you tried to get the candy or pennies?** (I wanted a lot of candy; I tried to grab as many as I could.)
- **If you could have anything in the world right now that would make you happy, what would it be?** (Answers will vary.)

Share: We always seem to want more and more stuff. And it's not easy to let go when we see something we want.

When hunters want to catch monkeys, they cut a hole in a small gourd just big enough for the monkey to get his hand in, place the food inside, and then attach the gourd to a tree. The monkey will reach in and grab the food but when he tries to pull his hand out, he cannot because it is too big with the handful of food. Instead of letting go of the food, he will stay tiring himself out until captured, because he will not let go of the food he wanted.

Sometimes we are like the monkey. We get so focused on things we want that we forget what is really important in life. Material things only bring temporary happiness.

Have family members each think of one thing that they know a friend has that is better than something they own. For example, someone might consider his relatively cheap baseball glove and compare it to a friend's fancy, expensive glove. Discuss:
- **How would having a better [baseball glove or whatever item you thought of] make you happy? How long would that happiness last?**

Age Adjustments

HERE'S A LESSON YOUNG CHILDREN can relate to. Even when children are quite young, they begin to covet things that other people have. You'll see this with toddlers who often make a beeline for a toy being played with by a peer. You can help to make this lesson more valuable to your younger children by teaching them to be happy with the toys they have. Spend a few minutes talking about some of their toys and how much they enjoy them. Ask what it might be like to not have any toys at all. Then encourage your younger children to be content with the many good things they've been given. Some young children will begin to think about friends who may not have much and may even offer to give up some of their toys as they realize the joy of giving to others.

• Do things bring us lasting happiness? Why or why not?

Share: When we compare what we have to what someone else has, we're setting ourselves up for disappointment. Wanting something that another person owns, or that we see in a store or catalog, is called coveting. The tenth commandment tells us it is wrong to covet or want things that we don't need or can't afford.

WRAP-UP

Gather everyone in a circle and have family members take turns answering this question: **What's one thing you've learned about God today?**

Next, tell kids you've got a new "Life Slogan" you'd like to share with them.

Life Slogan: Today's Life Slogan is this: "You shall not covet." Have family members repeat the slogan two or three times to help them learn it. Then encourage them to practice saying it during the week so they can talk about it at your next family night session.

Close in Prayer: Allow time for each family member to share prayer concerns and answers to prayer. Then close your time together with prayer for each concern. Thank God for listening to and caring about us.

Remember to record your prayer requests so you can refer to them in the future as you see God answering them.

How to Lead Your Child to Christ

SOME THINGS TO CONSIDER AHEAD OF TIME:

1. Realize that God is more concerned about your child's eternal destiny and happiness than you are. "The Lord is not slow in keeping His promise. . . . He is patient with you, not wanting anyone to perish, but everyone to come to repentance" (2 Peter 3:9).

2. Pray specifically beforehand that God will give you insights and wisdom in dealing with each child on his or her maturity level.

3. Don't use terms like "take Jesus into your heart," "dying and going to hell," and "accepting Christ as your personal Savior." Children are either too literal ("How does Jesus breathe in my heart?") or the words are too clichéd and trite for their understanding.

4. Deal with each child alone, and don't be in a hurry. Make sure he or she understands. Discuss. Take your time.

A FEW CAUTIONS:

1. When drawing children to Himself, Jesus said for others to "allow" them to come to Him (see Mark 10:14). Only with adults did He use the term "compel" (see Luke 14:23). Do not compel children.

2. Remember that unless the Holy Spirit is speaking to the child, there will be no genuine heart experience of regeneration. Parents, don't get caught up in the idea that Jesus will return the day before you were going to speak to your child about salvation and that it will be too late. Look at God's character—He *is* love! He is not dangling your child's soul over hell. Wait on God's timing.

   Pray with faith, believing. Be concerned, but don't push.

THE PLAN:

1. **God loves you.** Recite John 3:16 with your child's name in place of "the world."

2. **Show the child his or her need of a Savior.**

   a. Deal with sin carefully. There is one thing that cannot enter heaven—sin.

   b. Be sure your child knows what sin is. Ask him to name some (things common to children—lying, sassing, disobeying, etc.). Sin is doing or thinking anything wrong according to God's Word. It is breaking God's Law.

   c. Ask the question "Have you sinned?" If the answer is no, do not continue. Urge him to come and talk to you again when he does feel that he has sinned. Dismiss him. You may want to have prayer first, however, thanking God "for this young child who is willing to do what is right." Make it easy for him to talk to you again, but do not continue. Do not say, "Oh, yes, you have too sinned!" and then name some. With children, wait for God's conviction.

   d. If the answer is yes, continue. He may even give a personal illustration of some sin he has done recently or one that has bothered him.

   e. Tell him what God says about sin: We've all sinned ("There is no one righteous, not even one," Rom. 3:10). And because of that sin, we can't get to God ("For the wages of sin is death . . . " Rom. 6:23). So He had to come to us (". . . but the gift of God is eternal life in Christ Jesus our Lord," Rom. 6:23).

   f. Relate God's gift of salvation to Christmas gifts—we don't earn them or pay for them; we just accept them and are thankful for them.

3. **Bring the child to a definite decision.**

   a. Christ must be received if salvation is to be possessed.

   b. Remember, do not force a decision.

   c. Ask the child to pray out loud in her own words. Give her some things she could say if she seems unsure. Now be prepared for a blessing! (It is best to avoid having the child repeat a memorized prayer after you. Let her think, and make it personal.)*

d. After salvation has occurred, pray for her out loud. This is a good way to pronounce a blessing on her.

4. **Lead your child into assurance.**

Show him that he will have to keep his relationship open with God through repentance and forgiveness (just like with his family or friends), but that God will always love him ("Never will I leave you; never will I forsake you," Heb. 13:5).

* If you wish to guide your child through the prayer, here is some suggested language.

"Dear God, I know that I am a sinner [have child name specific sins he or she acknowledged earlier, such as lying, stealing, disobeying, etc.]. I know that Jesus died on the cross to pay for all my sins. I ask You to forgive me of my sins. I believe that Jesus died for me and rose from the dead, and I accept Him as my Savior. Thank You for loving me. In Jesus' name. Amen."

Cumulative Topical Index

TOPIC	SCRIPTURE	WHAT YOU'LL NEED	WHERE TO FIND IT
The Acts of the Sinful Nature and the Fruit of the Spirit	Gal. 5:19-26	3x5 cards or paper, markers, and tape	IFN, p. 43
Adding Value to Money through Saving Takes Time	Matt. 6:19-21	Supplies for making cookies and a Bible	MMK, p. 89
All Have Sinned	Rom. 3:23	Raw eggs, bucket of water	BCB, p. 89
All of Our Plans Should Match God's	Ps. 139:1-18	Paper, pencils, markers, or crayons	MMK, p. 73
Avoid Things That Keep Us from Growing	Eph. 4:14-15; Heb. 5:11-14	Seeds, plants at various stages of growth or a garden or nursery to tour, Bible	CCQ, p. 77
Bad Company Corrupts Good Character	1 Cor. 15:33	Small ball, string, slips of paper, pencil, yarn or masking tape, Bible	IFN, p. 103
Be Thankful for Good Friends		Bible, art supplies, markers	IFN, p. 98
Because We Love God, We Obey His Commands		Light source, variety of objects	TC, p. 23
Being Content with What We Have	Phil. 4:11-13	Bible	CCQ, p. 17
Being Diligent Means Working Hard and Well	Gen. 39–41	Bible, paper, a pencil and other supplies depending on jobs chosen	MMK, p. 64
Being a Faithful Steward Means Managing God's Gifts Wisely	1 Peter 4:10; Luke 19:12-26	Graham crackers, peanut butter, thin stick pretzels, small marshmallows, and M & Ms®	MMK, p. 18
Being Jealous Means Wanting Things Other People Have	Gen. 37:4-5	Different size boxes of candy or other treats, and a Bible	OTS, p. 39
Being with God in Heaven Is Worth More than Anything Else	Matt. 13:44-46	Hershey's kisses candies, a Bible	NTS, p. 24

TOPIC	SCRIPTURE	WHAT YOU'LL NEED	WHERE TO FIND IT
Budgeting Means Making a Plan for Using Our Money	Jud. 6–7	Table, large sheets or paper, and markers or crayons	MMK, p. 79
Budgeting Means the Money Coming in Has to Equal the Money Going Out	Luke 14:28-35; Jud. 6–7	Supply of beans, paper, pencil, and Bible	MMK, p. 80
By Setting Aside the Time to Focus on God, We Have a Chance to Reflect on His Glory and Goodness in Our "Busy" Lives	Mark 2:27; Heb. 12:1-4	Bible, poster board, crayons and or markers, a $5 bill, tape	TC, p. 49
Change Helps Us Grow and Mature	Rom. 8:28-39	Bible	WLS, p. 39
Change Is Good	1 Kings 17:8-16	Jar or box for holding change, colored paper, tape, markers, Bible	MMK, p. 27
Christ Is Who We Serve	Col. 3:23-24	Paper, scissors, pens	IFN, p. 50
The Christmas Story Is about Jesus' Birth	Luke 2; Matt. 2	Styrofoam cones and balls of various sizes, a large box, markers or paints, tape, a Bible	NTS, p. 47
Christians Should Be Joyful Each Day	James 3:22-23; Ps. 118:24	Small plastic bottle, cork to fit bottle opening, water, vinegar, paper towel, Bible	CCQ, p. 67
Commitment and Hard Work Are Needed to Finish Strong	Gen. 6:5-22	Jigsaw puzzle, Bible	CCQ, p. 83
The Consequence of Sin Is Death	Ps. 19:1-6	Dominoes	BCB, p. 57
Contentment Is the Secret to Happiness	Matt. 6:33	Package of candies, a Bible	MMK, p. 51
Creation	Gen. 1:1; Ps. 19:1-6; Rom. 1:20	Nature book or video, Bible	IFN, p. 17
David and Bathsheba	2 Sam. 11:1–12:14	Bible	BCB, p. 90
Description of Heaven	Rev. 21:3-4, 10-27	Bible, drawing supplies	BCB, p. 76
Difficulty Can Help Us Grow	Jer. 32:17; Luke 18:27	Bible, card game like Old Maid or Crazy Eights	CCQ, p. 33

TOPIC	SCRIPTURE	WHAT YOU'LL NEED	WHERE TO FIND IT
Discipline and Training Make Us Stronger	Prov. 4:23	Narrow doorway, Bible	CCQ, p. 103
Do Not Give In to Those Around You	Matt. 14:6-12; Luke 23:13-25	Empty one two-liter plastic bottles, eye-dropper, water, a Bible	SS, p.21
Don't Be Distracted by Unimportant Things	Matt. 14:22-32	One marked penny, lots of unmarked pennies, a wrapped gift for each child, a Bible	NTS, p. 35
Don't Be Yoked with Unbelievers	2 Cor. 16:17–17:1	Milk, food coloring	IFN, p. 105
Don't Give Respect Based on Material Wealth	Eph. 6:1-8; 1 Peter 2:13-17; Ps. 119:17; James 2:1-2; 1 Tim. 4:12	Large sheet of paper, tape, a pen, Bible	IFN, p. 64
Dorcas Made Clothes and Did Good Things	Acts 9:36-42	Large pillowcases, fabric markers, scissors, a Bible	NTS, p. 71
Easter Was God's Plan for Jesus	John 3:16; Rom. 3:23; 6:23	Paper and pencils or pens, materials to make a large cross, and a Bible	HFN, p. 27
Equality Does Not Mean Contentment	Matt. 20:1-16	Money or candy bars, tape recorder or radio, Bible	WLS, p. 21
Even if We're Not in the Majority, We May Be Right	2 Tim. 3:12-17	Piece of paper, pencil, water	CCQ, p. 95
Every Day Is a Gift from God	Prov. 16:9	Bible	CCQ, p. 69
Evil Hearts Say Evil Words	Prov. 15:2-8; Luke 6:45; Eph. 4:29	Bible, small mirror	IFN, p. 79
Family Members Ought to Be Loyal to Each Other	The Book of Ruth	Shoebox, two pieces of different colored felt, seven pipe cleaners (preferably of different colors)	OTS, p. 67
The Fruit of the Spirit	Gal. 5:22-23; Luke 3:8; Acts 26:20	Blindfold and Bible	BCB, p. 92
God Allows Testing to Help Us Mature	James 1:2-4	Bible	BCB, p. 44
God Became a Man So We Could Understand His Love	John 14:9-10	A pet of some kind, and a Bible	HFN, p. 85
God Can Clean Our Guilty Consciences	1 John 1:9	Small dish of bleach, dark piece of material, Bible	WLS, p. 95

TOPIC	SCRIPTURE	WHAT YOU'LL NEED	WHERE TO FIND IT
God Can Do the Impossible	John 6:1-14	Bible, sturdy plank (6 or more inches wide and 6 to 8 feet long), a brick or similar object, snack of fish and crackers	CCQ, p. 31
God Can Give Us Strength		Musical instruments (or pots and pans with wooden spoons) and a snack	OTS, p. 52
God Can Guide Us Away from Satan's Traps	Ps. 119:9-11; Prov. 3:5-6	Ten or more inexpensive mousetraps, pencil, blindfold, Bible	WLS, p. 72
God Can Help Us Knock Sin Out of Our Lives	Ps. 32:1-5; 1 John 1:9	Heavy drinking glass, pie tin, small slips of paper, pencils, large raw egg, cardboard tube from a roll of toilet paper, broom, masking tape, Bible	WLS, p. 53
God Can Use Us in Unique Ways to Accomplish His Plans		Strings of cloth, clothespins or strong tape, "glow sticks" or small flashlights	OTS, p. 63
God Cares for Us Even in Hard Times	Job 1–2; 42	Bible	WLS, p. 103
God Chose to Make Dads (or Moms) as a Picture of Himself	Gen. 1:26-27	Large sheets of paper, pencils, a bright light, a picture of your family, a Bible	HFN, p. 47
God Commands Honoring for Our Benefit	Luke 15:11-32; Ex. 20:12; Deut. 5:16	Bibles	TC, p. 56
God Created the Heavens and the Earth	Gen. 1	Small tent or sheet and a rope, Christmas lights, two buckets (one with water), a coffee can with dirt, a tape recorder and cassette, and a flashlight	OTS, p. 17
God Created Us	Isa. 45:9, 64:8; Ps. 139:13	Bible and video of potter with clay	BCB, p. 43
God Created the World, Stars, Plants, Animals, and People	Gen. 1	Play dough or clay, safe shaping or cutting tools, a Bible	OTS, p. 19
God Doesn't Want Us to Worry	Matt. 6:25-34; Phil. 4:6-7; Ps. 55:22	Bible, paper, pencils	CCQ, p. 39

TOPIC	SCRIPTURE	WHAT YOU'LL NEED	WHERE TO FIND IT
God Forgives Those Who Confess Their Sins	1 John 1:9	Sheets of paper, tape, Bible	BCB, p. 58
God Gave Jesus a Message for Us	John 1:14,18; 8:19; 12:49-50	Goldfish in water or bug in jar, water	BCB, p. 66
God Gives and God Can Take Away	Luke 12:13-21	Bible, timer with bell or buzzer, large bowl of small candies, smaller bowl for each child	CCQ, p. 15
God Gives Us the Skills We Need to Do What He Asks of Us		Materials to make a sling (cloth, shoe-strings), plastic golf balls or marshmal-lows, stuffed animals	OTS, p. 73
God Is Holy	Ex. 3:1-6	Masking tape, baby powder or corn starch, broom, Bible	IFN, p. 31
God Is Invisible, Powerful, and Real	John 1:18, 4:24; Luke 24:36-39	Balloons, balls, refrigerator magnets, Bible	IFN, p. 15
God Is the Source of Our Strength	Jud. 16	Oversized sweat-shirt, balloons, mop heads or other items to use as wigs, items to stack to make pillars, a Bible	OTS, p. 61
God Is Our Only Source of Strength	Isa. 40:29-31	Straws, fresh baking potatoes, a Bible	SS, p.33
God Is with Us	Ex. 25:10-22; Deut. 10:1-5; Josh. 3:14-17; 1 Sam. 3:3; 2 Sam. 6:12-15	A large cardboard box, two broom han-dles, a utility knife, strong tape, gold spray paint, and a Bible	OTS, p. 49
God Keeps His Promises	Gen. 6–9:16	Plastic coffee can lid, flashlight, bubble solution, straw, a Bible	SS, p.75
God Keeps His Promises	Gen. 9:13, 15	Sheets of colored cel-lophane, cardboard, scissors, tape, a Bible, a lamp or large flashlight	OTS, p. 25
God Knew His Plans for Us	Jer. 29:11	Two puzzles and a Bible	BCB, p. 19
God Knew Moses Would Be Found by Pharaoh's Daughter	Ex. 2:1-10	A doll or stuffed animal, a basket, and a blanket	OTS, p. 43
God Knows All about Us	Ps. 139:2-4; Matt. 10:30	3x5 cards, a pen	BCB, p. 17

TOPIC	SCRIPTURE	WHAT YOU'LL NEED	WHERE TO FIND IT
God Knows Everything	Isa. 40:13-14; Eph. 4:1-6	Bible	IFN, p. 15
God Knows the Plan for Our Lives	Rom. 8:28	Three different 25–50 piece jigsaw puzzles, Bible	WLS, p. 101
God Looks at the Heart	1 Sam. 16:7; Gal. 2:6	4 cans of pop (2 regular and 2 diet), 1 large tub, duct tape, water, a Bible	SS, p. 81
God Looks beyond the Mask and into Our Hearts		Costumes	HFN, p. 65
God Loves and Protects Us	Matt. 6:26-27	One or two raw eggs, a sink or bucket, a Bible	SS, p. 15
God Loves Us So Much, He Sent Jesus	John 3:16; Eph. 2:8-9	I.O.U. for each family member	IFN, p. 34
God Made Our Family Unique by Placing Each of Us in It		Different color paint for each family member, toothpicks or paintbrushes to dip into paint, white paper, Bible	BCB, p. 110
God Made Us		Building blocks, such as Tinkertoys, Legos, or K'nex	HFN, p. 15
God Made Us in His Image	Gen. 1:24-27	Play dough or clay and Bible	BCB, p. 24
God Never Changes	Ecc. 3:1-8; Heb. 13:8	Paper, pencils, Bible	WLS, p. 37
God Owns Everything; He Gives Us Things to Manage		Large sheet of poster board or newsprint and colored markers	MMK, p. 17
God Provides a Way Out of Temptation	1 Cor. 10:12-13; James 1:13-14; 4:7; 1 John 2:15-17	Bible	IFN, p. 88
God Sees Who We Really Are—We Can Never Fool Him	1 Sam. 16:7	Construction paper, scissors, crayons or markers, a hat or bowl, and a Bible	HFN, p. 66
God Strengthens Us and Protects Us from Satan	2 Thes. 3:3; Ps. 18:2-3	Two un-inflated black balloons, water, a candle, matches, a Bible	SS, p. 16
God Teaches Us about Love through Others	1 Cor. 13	Colored paper, markers, crayons, scissors, tape or glue, and a Bible	HFN, p. 22

Family Night
TOOL CHEST

AN INTRODUCTION TO FAMILY NIGHTS
= IFN

BASIC CHRISTIAN BELIEFS
= BCB

CHRISTIAN CHARACTER QUALITIES
= CCQ

WISDOM LIFE SKILLS
= WLS

MONEY MATTERS FOR KIDS
= MMK

HOLIDAYS FAMILY NIGHT
= HFN

BIBLE STORIES FOR PRESCHOOLERS (OLD TESTAMENT)
= OTS

SIMPLE SCIENCE
= SS

BIBLE STORIES FOR PRESCHOOLERS (NEW TESTAMENT)
= NTS

TEN COMMANDMENTS
= TC

TOPIC	SCRIPTURE	WHAT YOU'LL NEED	WHERE TO FIND IT
God Used Plagues to Tell Pharaoh to Let Moses and His People Go	Ex. 7–12	A clear glass, red food coloring, water, and a Bible	OTS, p. 44
God Uses Many Ways to Get Our Attention	Dan. 5	Large sheets of paper or poster board, tape, finger-paint, and a Bible	OTS, p. 79
God Wants Our Best Effort in All We Do	Col. 3:23-24	Children's blocks or a large supply of cardboard boxes	MMK, p. 63
God Wants a Passionate Relationship with Us	Rev. 3:16	Pans of hot, cold, and lukewarm water, hot and cold drinks	SS, p. 69
God Wants Us to Be Diligent in Our Work	Prov. 6:6-11; 1 Thes. 4:11-12	Video about ants or picture books or encyclopedia, Bible	CCQ, p. 55
God Wants Us to Get Closer to Him	James 4:8; 1 John 4:7-12	Hidden Bibles, clues to find them	BCB, p. 33
God Wants Us to Give to Others in Love		Candy	NTS, p. 54
God Wants Us to Glorify Him	Ps. 24:1; Luke 12:13-21	Paper, pencils, Bible	WLS, p. 47
God Wants Us to Reflect His Word	James 1:19-25	Bible, hand mirror, cardboard, a flashlight	NTS, p. 84
God Wants Us to Work and Be Helpful	2 Thes. 3:6-15	Several undone chores, Bible	CCQ, p. 53
God Will Never Leave Us or Forsake Us	Matt. 28:20	Long sheet of paper, pencil, scissors, tape or glue, a Bible	SS, p. 76
God Will Send the Holy Spirit	John 14:23-26; 1 Cor. 2:12	Flashlights, small treats, Bible	IFN, p. 39
God Will Separate Those Who Believe in Jesus from Those Who Don't	Matt. 13:47-49; John 3:16	Large box, crayons or markers, a large bath towel, candy-size rocks, candy, wax paper, a Bible	NTS, p. 29
God Will Separate Those Who Love Him from Those Who Don't	Matt. 25:31-46	Coarse salt, ground pepper, plastic spoon, wool cloth, a Bible	SS, p. 64
God's Covenant with Noah	Gen. 8:13-21; 9:8-17	Bible, paper, crayons or markers	BCB, p. 52
God's Name Represents His Character, Person-age, Nature, Reputa-tion, and Role	Ex. 20:7; Matt. 5:34	Dictionary, paper, pencils, a Bible	TC, p. 41

TOPIC	SCRIPTURE	WHAT YOU'LL NEED	WHERE TO FIND IT
A Good Friend Encourages Us to Do What Jesus Would Do	Ecc. 4:9-12	Strips of cardboard, books, 50 pennies, a Bible	SS, p. 82
Guarding the Gate to Our Minds	Prov. 4:13; 2 Cor. 11:3; Phil. 4:8	Bible, poster board for each family member, old magazines, glue, scissors, markers	CCQ, p. 23
The Holy Spirit Helps Us	Eph. 1:17; John 14:15-17; Acts 1:1-11; Eph. 3:16-17; Rom. 8:26-27; 1 Cor. 2:11-16	Bible	BCB, p. 99
The Holy Spirit Helps Us to Be a Light in the Dark World	Matt. 5:14-16; 1 Tim. 2:1-4	Wintergreen or Cryst-O-Mint Lifesavers, a Bible	SS, p. 40
Honesty Means Being Sure We Tell the Truth and Are Fair	Prov. 10:9; 11:3; 12:5; 14:2; 28:13	A bunch of coins and a Bible	MMK, p. 58
Honor the Holy Spirit, Don't Block Him	1 John 4:4; 1 Cor. 6:19-20	Bible, blow-dryer or vacuum cleaner with exit hose, a Ping-Pong ball	CCQ, p. 47
Honor Your Parents	Ex. 20:12	Paper, pencil, treats, umbrella, soft objects, masking tape, pen, Bible	IFN, p. 55
Honoring Your Parents Teaches You to Honor God		Balloon, two different pieces of colored paper, pencils	TC, p. 55
How Big Is an Ark?		Large open area, buckets of water, cans of animal food, bags of dog food, and four flags	OTS, p. 24
Idols Come in All Shapes and Sizes	Isa. 46:1-11; Col. 3:5-6	A favorite thing from each child	TC, p. 37
If We Accept Jesus as Savior, We'll Get into Heaven	Rev. 20:15, 21:27	Bible, marshmallows, cotton candy, ice cream	NTS, p. 90
If We Confess Our Sins, Jesus Will Forgive Us	Heb. 12:1;1 John 1:9	Magic slate, candies, paper, pencils, bathrobe ties or soft rope, items to weigh someone down, and a Bible	HFN, p. 28
Intent to Commit Sexual Sin Is as Wrong as the Act Itself	Matt. 5:27-28; Ps. 119:9	Three large boxes and a Bible	TC, p. 69

Family Night
TOOL CHEST

AN INTRODUCTION TO FAMILY NIGHTS
= IFN

BASIC CHRISTIAN BELIEFS
= BCB

CHRISTIAN CHARACTER QUALITIES
= CCQ

WISDOM LIFE SKILLS
= WLS

MONEY MATTERS FOR KIDS
= MMK

HOLIDAYS FAMILY NIGHT
= HFN

BIBLE STORIES FOR PRESCHOOLERS (OLD TESTAMENT)
= OTS

SIMPLE SCIENCE
= SS

BIBLE STORIES FOR PRESCHOOLERS (NEW TESTAMENT)
= NTS

TEN COMMANDMENTS
= TC

TOPIC	SCRIPTURE	WHAT YOU'LL NEED	WHERE TO FIND IT
Investing and Saving Adds Value to Money	Prov. 21:20	Two and a half dollars for each family member	MMK, p. 87
It Is Important to Spend Time Praising God	Ps. 66:1; 81:1; 95:1; 98:4; 100:1	Plastic straws, scissors, a Bible	SS, p. 52
It's Better to Follow the Truth	Rom. 1:25; Prov. 2:1-5	Second set of clues, box of candy or treats, Bible	WLS, p. 86
It's Better to Wait for Something Than to Borrow Money to Buy It	2 Kings 4:1-7; Prov. 22:7	Magazines, advertisements, paper, a pencil, Bible	MMK, p. 103
It's Difficult to Be a Giver When You're a Debtor		Pennies or other coins	MMK, p. 105
It's Easy to Follow a Lie, but It Leads to Disappointment		Clues as described in lesson, empty box	WLS, p. 85
The Importance of Your Name Being Written in the Book of Life	Rev. 20:11-15; 21:27	Bible, phone book, access to other books with family name	BCB, p. 74
It's Important to Listen to Jesus' Message		Bible	BCB, p. 68
It's Not Always Easy to Do What Jesus Wants Us to Do	Matt. 7:13	Toy blocks, a narrow board, two cinder blocks, a Bible	NTS, p. 17
It's Not Easy to Break a Pattern of Sin	James 1:12-15	Paper, pan, water, a Bible	SS, p. 63
Jesus Came to Die for Our Sins	Rom. 5:8	A large piece of cardboard, markers, scissors, tape, and a Bible	HFN, p. 91
Jesus Came to Give Us Eternal Life	Mark 16:12-14	A calculator, a calendar, a sheet of paper, and a pencil	HFN, p. 91
Jesus Came to Teach Us about God	John 1:14, 18	Winter clothing, bread crumbs, a Bible	HFN, p. 92
Jesus Came to Show Us How Much God Loves Us	John 3:16	Supplies to make an Advent wreath, and a Bible	HFN, p. 89
Jesus Comes to Find Us When We Are Lost	Luke 15:1-7	Bible, blindfolds	NTS, p. 61
Jesus Cried Just Like We Do	John 11	Children's Bible storybook, a Bible, or video, *The Easter Promise*	NTS, p. 65

TOPIC	SCRIPTURE	WHAT YOU'LL NEED	WHERE TO FIND IT
Jesus Died for Our Sins	Luke 22:1-6; Mark 14:12-26; Luke 22:47-54; Luke 22:55-62; Matt. 27:1-10; Matt. 27:11-31; Luke 23:26-34	Seven plastic eggs, slips of paper with Scripture verses, and a Bible	HFN, p. 33
Jesus Dies on the Cross	John 14:6	6-foot 2x4, 3-foot 2x4, hammers, nails, Bible	IFN, p. 33
Jesus Has Power over Death		Toilet paper rolls	NTS, p. 66
Jesus Promises Us New Bodies and a New Home in Heaven	Phil. 3:20-21; Luke 24:36-43; Rev. 21:1-4	Ingredients for making pumpkin pie, and a Bible	HFN, p. 61
Jesus Took Our Sins to the Cross and Freed Us from Being Bound Up in Sin	Rom. 6:23, 5:8; 6:18	Soft rope or heavy yarn, a watch with a second hand, thread, and a Bible	HFN, p. 53
Jesus Took the Punishment We Deserve	Rom. 6:23; John 3:16; Rom. 5:8-9	Bathrobe, list of bad deeds	IFN, p. 26
Jesus Wants Us to Do the Right Thing			NTS, p. 18
Jesus Was Victorious Over Death and Sin	Luke 23:35-43; Luke 23:44-53; Matt. 27:59-61; Luke 23:54–24:12	Five plastic eggs— four with Scripture verses, and a Bible	HFN, p. 36
Jesus Washes His Followers' Feet	John 13:1-17	Bucket of warm soapy water, towels, Bible	IFN, p. 63
Joshua and the Battle of Jericho	Josh. 1:16-18; 6:1-21	Paper, pencil, dots on paper that, when connected, form a star	IFN, p. 57
Knowing God's Word Helps Us Know What Stand to Take	2 Tim. 3:1-5	Current newspaper, Bible	CCQ, p. 93
Look to God, Not Others	Phil. 4:11-13	Magazines or newspapers, a chair, several pads of small yellow stickies, Bible	WLS, p. 24
Love Is Unselfish	1 Cor. 13	A snack and a Bible	HFN, p. 21
Love Means Putting Others' Needs above Our Own	Luke 10:25-37	Children's Bible storybook, two equal-length strips of wood, paper, marker, costumes, a Bible	NTS, p. 53

Family Night
TOOL CHEST

AN INTRODUCTION TO FAMILY NIGHTS
= IFN

BASIC CHRISTIAN BELIEFS
= BCB

CHRISTIAN CHARACTER QUALITIES
= CCQ

WISDOM LIFE SKILLS
= WLS

MONEY MATTERS FOR KIDS
= MMK

HOLIDAYS FAMILY NIGHT
= HFN

BIBLE STORIES FOR PRESCHOOLERS (OLD TESTAMENT)
= OTS

SIMPLE SCIENCE
= SS

BIBLE STORIES FOR PRESCHOOLERS (NEW TESTAMENT)
= NTS

TEN COMMANDMENTS
= TC

TOPIC	SCRIPTURE	WHAT YOU'LL NEED	WHERE TO FIND IT
Loving Money Is Wrong	1 Tim. 6:6-10	Several rolls of coins, masking tape, Bible	WLS, p. 45
Lying Can Hurt People	Acts 5:1-11	Two pizza boxes—one empty and one with a fresh pizza—and a Bible	MMK, p. 57
Lying Has Consequences	Ex. 20:16; Matt. 5:37	Baseball bat or stick of same length, masking tape, Bible	TC, p. 81
Meeting Goals Requires Planning	Prov. 3:5-6	Paper, scissors, pencils, a treat, a Bible	MMK, p. 71
Moms Are Special and Important to Us and to God	Prov. 24:3-4	Confetti, streamers, a comfortable chair, a wash basin with warm water, two cloths, and a Bible	HFN, p. 41
Moms Model Jesus' Love When They Serve Gladly	2 Tim. 1:4-7	Various objects depending on chosen activity and a Bible	HFN, p. 42
The More We Know God, the More We Know His Voice	John 10:1-6	Bible	BCB, p. 35
Murders, and the Attitude that Causes People to Murder, Is Sinful	Ex. 20:13; Matt. 22:37-39; Gen. 4:8-10	Pennies and a Bible	TC, p. 61
Nicodemus Asks Jesus about Being Born Again	John 3:7, 50-51; 19:39-40	Bible, paper, pencil, costume	BCB, p. 81
Noah Obeyed God When He Built the Ark	Gen. 6:14-16	A large refrigerator box, markers or paints, self-adhesive paper, stuffed animals, a Bible, utility knife	OTS, p. 23
Nothing Is Impossible When It Is in God's Will	Matt. 21:28	Hard-boiled egg, butter, glass bottle, paper, matches, a Bible	SS, p. 34
Obedience Has Good Rewards		Planned outing everyone will enjoy, directions on 3x5 cards, number cards	IFN, p. 59
Obey God First		Paper, markers, scissors, and blindfolds	OTS, p. 80

TOPIC	SCRIPTURE	WHAT YOU'LL NEED	WHERE TO FIND IT
Only a Relationship with God Can Fill Our Need	Isa. 55:1-2	Doll that requires batteries, batteries for the doll, dollar bill, pictures of a house, an expensive car, and a pretty woman or handsome man, Bible	WLS, p. 62
Only God Can Provide for Our Needs	Ex. 20:4-6	Items representing children's favorite media stars and a Bible	TC, p. 35
Our Actions Should Mirror God, Not the World	Rom. 12:2	Regular glass, dried peas, a wine glass, a pie tin, water, a Bible	SS, p. 57
Our Conscience Helps Us Know Right from Wrong	Rom. 2:14-15	Foods with a strong smell, blindfold, Bible	WLS, p. 93
Our Minds Should Be Filled with Good, Not Evil	Phil 4:8; Ps. 119:9, 11	Bible, bucket of water, several large rocks	CCQ, p. 26
Our Tongue Is Powerful and Should Be Used to Glorify God	James 3:5-8	Squirt gun, pie pan, Pop Rocks candy, a Bible	SS, p. 51
Parable of the Talents	Matt. 25:14-30	Bible	IFN, p. 73
Parable of the Vine and Branches	John 15:1-8	Tree branch, paper, pencils, Bible	IFN, p. 95
People Came to See Jesus and Bring Him Gifts	Luke 2; Matt. 2	Styrofoam cones and balls of various sizes, a large box, markers or paints, tape, a Bible	NTS, p. 48
People, Like Plants, Need Good Soil to Grow	Mark 4:3-8, 13-20	Cake pan, aluminum foil, small stones, seeds, toothpicks, potting soil, a Bible	NTS, p. 41
People Look at Outside Appearance, but God Looks at the Heart	1 Sam. 17	Slings from activity on p. 73, plastic golf balls or marshmallows, a tape measure, cardboard, markers, and a Bible	OTS, p. 75
People Who Have the Gift of Hospitality Open Their Homes and Serve Others		Snacks and supplies for a nice meal	NTS, p. 78
Persecution Brings a Reward		Bucket, bag of ice, marker, one-dollar bill	WLS, p. 32

Family Night
TOOL CHEST

AN INTRODUCTION TO FAMILY NIGHTS
= IFN

BASIC CHRISTIAN BELIEFS
= BCB

CHRISTIAN CHARACTER QUALITIES
= CCQ

WISDOM LIFE SKILLS
= WLS

MONEY MATTERS FOR KIDS
= MMK

HOLIDAYS FAMILY NIGHT
= HFN

BIBLE STORIES FOR PRESCHOOLERS (OLD TESTAMENT)
= OTS

SIMPLE SCIENCE
= SS

BIBLE STORIES FOR PRESCHOOLERS (NEW TESTAMENT)
= NTS

TEN COMMANDMENTS
= TC

TOPIC	SCRIPTURE	WHAT YOU'LL NEED	WHERE TO FIND IT
Planning Helps Us Finish Strong	Phil. 3:10-14	Flight map on p. 86, paper, pencils, Bible	CCQ, p. 85
Pray, Endure, and Be Glad When We're Persecuted	Matt. 5:11-12, 44; Rom. 12:14; 1 Cor. 4:12	Notes, Bible, candle or flashlight, dark small space	WLS, p. 29
Priscilla Had the Gift of Hospitality	Acts 18:1-4, 18-26; Rom. 16:3-5	Large sheet, rope, clothespins, a Bible	NTS, p. 77
Putting God First Builds a Solid Relationship	Mark 6:35; Luke 4:16; Mark 13:31; Luke 12:31	Wide-mouth glass jar, large rocks, sand, water, permanent marker, a Bible	SS, p. 70
Remember All God Has Done for You	Ex. 25:1; 16:34; Num. 17:10; Deut. 31:26	Ark of the covenant from p. 49, cardboard or Styrofoam, crackers, a stick, and a Bible	OTS, p. 51
Remember What God Has Done for You	Gen. 12:7-8; 13:18; 22:9	Bricks or large rocks, paint, and a Bible	OTS, p. 31
The Responsibilities of Families	Eph. 5:22-33; 6:1-4	Photo albums, Bible	BCB, p. 101
Satan Looks for Ways to Trap Us	Luke 4:1-13	Cardboard box, string, stick, small ball, Bible	WLS, p. 69
Self-control Helps Us Resist the Enemy	1 Peter 5:8-9; 1 Peter 2:11-12	Blindfold, watch or timer, feather or other "tickly" item, Bible	CCQ, p. 101
Serve One Another in Love	Gal. 5:13	Bag of small candies, at least three per child	IFN, p. 47
Sex Was Given to Adults as a Gift to Be Enjoyed Only in Marriage, as a True Sign of Commitment and Trust	1 Thes. 4:3-8; Ex. 20:4-6	Child's favorite wrapped candy, masking tape, a Bible	TC, p. 67
Share God's Love with Others So They Can Join Us in Heaven		Rocks, plastic bags, paper, pencils	NTS, p. 30
Sin and Busyness Interfere with Our Prayers	Luke 10:38-42; Ps. 46:10; Matt. 5:23-24; 1 Peter 3:7	Bible, two paper cups, two paper clips, long length of fishing line	CCQ, p. 61
Sin Separates Humanity	Gen. 3:1-24	Bible, clay creations, piece of hardened clay or play dough	BCB, p. 25
Some Places Aren't Open to Everyone		Book or magazine with "knock-knock" jokes	BCB, p. 73

TOPIC	SCRIPTURE	WHAT YOU'LL NEED	WHERE TO FIND IT
Some Things in Life Are Out of Our Control		Blindfolds	BCB, p. 41
Sometimes God Surprises Us with Great Things	Gen. 15:15	Large sheet of poster board, straight pins or straightened paper clips, a flashlight, and a Bible	OTS, p. 32
Sometimes We Face Things That Seem Impossible		Bunch of cardboard boxes or blocks	OTS, p. 55
Stand Strong in the Lord	Prov. 1:8-10; 12:3	A jar, string, chair, fan, small weight, a Bible	SS, p. 22
Temptation Takes Our Eyes Off God		Fishing pole, items to catch, timer, Bible	IFN, p. 85
The Ten Commandments Are the Standards for How God Wants Us to Live		Target with 10 holes, balls, bean bags or rolled socks	TC, p. 15
The Ten Commandments Help Us to Identify What Sin Is in Today's World	Ex. 20	Paper, pens or pencils, and a Bible	TC, p. 21
The Ten Commandments Show Us Our Sinfulness and Our Need for a Savior	Rom. 3:20; 7:7-20	Butcher paper, pens, measuring tape, and a Bible	TC, p. 17
Test What the World Offers for Consistency with Jesus' Teachings	1 John 4:1	Candle, apple, almond, a Bible	SS, p. 58
There Are Only Two Things That Will Last, People (Relationships) and God's Word	Matt. 6:33	Paper, markers, a Bible	TC, p. 87
There Is a Difference between Needs and Wants	Prov. 31:16; Matt. 6:21	Paper, pencils, glasses of drinking water, a soft drink	MMK, p. 95
There Is Only One True God We Can Trust and Believe In	Ex. 20:3	Small cups that look identical, a small object (such as a ball), a Bible	TC, p. 27
Things That Are Important to Us Don't Always Cost a Lot of money		Stuffed toy, candy bar, toys, etc.	NTS, p. 23
Those Who Don't Believe Are Foolish	Ps. 44:1	Ten small pieces of paper, pencil, Bible	IFN, p. 19

Family Night
TOOL CHEST

AN
INTRODUCTION
TO FAMILY
NIGHTS
= IFN

BASIC
CHRISTIAN
BELIEFS
= BCB

CHRISTIAN
CHARACTER
QUALITIES
= CCQ

WISDOM LIFE
SKILLS
= WLS

MONEY
MATTERS FOR
KIDS
= MMK

HOLIDAYS
FAMILY NIGHT
= HFN

BIBLE STORIES
FOR
PRESCHOOLERS
(OLD TESTAMENT)
= OTS

SIMPLE
SCIENCE
= SS

BIBLE STORIES
FOR
PRESCHOOLERS
(NEW TESTAMENT)
= NTS

TEN
COMMANDMENTS
= TC

TOPIC	SCRIPTURE	WHAT YOU'LL NEED	WHERE TO FIND IT
A Time of Rest Helps Us to Refocus on God and Brings Purpose to All Our Weekly Activity— to Serve Him	Gen. 2:2-3; Ex. 20:8-11; 31:12-17	Bible, balloons, markers, 1 small stone per child, paper, and pencils	TC, p. 47
Tithing Means Giving One-Tenth Back to God	Gen. 28:10-22; Ps. 3:9-10	All family members need ten similar items each, a Bible	MMK, p. 33
To Get to Heaven, Your Name Must Be in the Book of Life		Phone book, paper, crayons or markers	NTS, p. 89
The Tongue Is Small but Powerful	James 3:3-12	Video, news magazine or picture book showing devastation of fire, match, candle, Bible	IFN, p. 77
The Treasure of a Thankful Heart Is Contentment	Eph. 5:20	3x5 cards, pencils, fun prizes, and a Bible	HFN, p. 72
Trials Help Us Grow	James 1:2-4	Sugar cookie dough, cookie cutters, baking sheets, miscellaneous baking supplies, Bible	WLS, p. 15
Trials Test How We've Grown	James 1:12	Bible	WLS, p. 17
Trust Is Important	Matt. 6:25-34	Each person needs an item he or she greatly values	MMK, p. 25
Truth Is the Opposite of Lying, and God Is Truth	Matt. 12:36-37	Two magnets, a Bible	TC, p. 83
We All Have Weaknesses and Will Be Attacked by Satan	1 Kings 11:3-4; 2 Cor. 12:9-10	Two pieces of plain white paper, a pencil, a Bible	SS, p. 28
We All Sin	Rom. 3:23	Target and items to throw	IFN, p. 23
We Are a Family for Life, Forever	Ruth 1:4	Shoebox; scissors; paper or cloth; magnets; photos of family members, friends, others; and a Bible	OTS, p. 68
We Are Made in God's Image	Gen. 2:7; Ps. 139:13-16	Paper bags, candies, a Bible, supplies for making gingerbread cookies	HFN, p. 17
We Become a New Creation When Jesus Comes into Our Hearts	Matt. 23:25-28; Rev. 3:20; 2 Cor. 5:17; Eph. 2:10; 2 Cor. 4:7-10; Matt. 5:14-16; 2 Cor. 4:6	Pumpkin, newspaper, sharp knife, a spoon, a candle, matches, and a Bible	HFN, p. 59

TOPIC	SCRIPTURE	WHAT YOU'LL NEED	WHERE TO FIND IT
We Can Communicate with Each Other			BCB, p. 65
We Can Do Good Things for Others	1 Cor. 13:4	Newsprint or a large sheet of paper, markers or crayons, children's clothing, money to buy new clothes, a Bible	NTS, p. 72
We Can Fight the Temptation to Want More Stuff	Matt. 4:1-11; Heb. 13:5	Television, paper, a pencil, Bible	MMK, p. 49
We Can Give Joyfully to Others	Luke 10:25-37	Bible, soft yarn	MMK, p. 41
We Can Help Each Other	Prov. 27:17	Masking tape, bowl of unwrapped candies, rulers, yardsticks, or dowel rods	BCB, p. 110
We Can Help People When We Give Generously	2 Cor. 6–7	Variety of supplies, depending on chosen activity	MMK, p. 43
We Can Learn about God from Mom (or Dad)		Supplies to make a collage (magazines, paper, tape or glue, scissors)	HFN, p. 49
We Can Learn and Grow from Good and Bad Situations	Gen. 37–48; Rom. 8:29	A Bible and a camera (optional)	OTS, p. 37
We Can Love by Helping Those in Need	Heb. 13:1-3		IFN, p. 48
We Can Show Love through Respecting Family Members		Paper and pen	IFN, p. 66
We Can't Hide from God		Supplies will vary	OTS, p. 85
We Can't Take Back the Damage of Our Words		Tube of toothpaste for each child, $10 bill	IFN, p. 78
We Deserve Punishment for Our Sins	Rom. 6:23	Dessert, other materials as decided	IFN, p. 24
We Give to God because We're Thankful		Supplies for a celebration dinner, also money for each family member	MMK, p. 36
We Have All We Need in Our Lives	Ecc. 3:11	Paper, pencils, Bible	WLS, p. 61

Family Night
TOOL CHEST

AN INTRODUCTION TO FAMILY NIGHTS
= IFN

BASIC CHRISTIAN BELIEFS
= BCB

CHRISTIAN CHARACTER QUALITIES
= CCQ

WISDOM LIFE SKILLS
= WLS

MONEY MATTERS FOR KIDS
= MMK

HOLIDAYS FAMILY NIGHT
= HFN

BIBLE STORIES FOR PRESCHOOLERS (OLD TESTAMENT)
= OTS

SIMPLE SCIENCE
= SS

BIBLE STORIES FOR PRESCHOOLERS (NEW TESTAMENT)
= NTS

TEN COMMANDMENTS
= TC

TOPIC	SCRIPTURE	WHAT YOU'LL NEED	WHERE TO FIND IT
We Have a New Life in Christ	John 3:3; 2 Cor. 5:17	Video or picture book of caterpillar forming a cocoon then a butterfly, or a tadpole becoming a frog, or a seed becoming a plant	BCB, p. 93
We Have Much to Be Thankful For	1 Chron. 16:4-36	Unpopped popcorn, a bowl, supplies for popping popcorn, and a Bible	HFN, p. 79
We Know Others by Our Relationships with Them		Copies of question-naire, pencils, Bible	BCB, p. 31
We Must Be in Constant Contact with God		Blindfold	CCQ, p. 63
We Must Choose to Obey		3x5 cards or slips of paper, markers, and tape	IFN, p. 43
We Must Either Choose Christ or Reject Christ	Matt. 12:30	Clear glass jar, cooking oil, water, spoon, Bible	CCQ, p. 96
We Must Give Thanks in All Circumstances	1 Thes. 5:18	A typical family meal, cloth strips, and a Bible	HFN, p. 77
We Must Hold Firm to Our Faith and Depend on God for Strength	Eph. 6:16	Balloons, long darts or shish kebab skewers, cooking oil, a Bible	SS, p. 27
We Must Learn How Much Responsibility We Can Handle		Building blocks, watch with second hand, paper, pencil	IFN, p. 71
We Must Listen	Prov. 1:5, 8-9; 4:1	Bible, other supplies for the task you choose	WLS, p. 77
We Must "Root" Ourselves in Jesus and Live by God's Word	Mark 4:1-24	A potted plant, light-weight cardboard, crayons, scissors, a Bible	NTS, p. 42
We Must Stay Focused on Jesus So We Don't Fall		Masking tape	NTS, p. 36
We Must Think Before We Speak	James 1:19	Bible	WLS, p. 79
We Need to Feed on God's Word to Grow in Christ	Ps. 119:105; 2 Chron. 34:31; Acts 17:11; James 1:22-25	Raisins, clear drink-ing glass, a two-liter bottle of clear soft drink, a Bible	SS, p. 46

TOPIC	SCRIPTURE	WHAT YOU'LL NEED	WHERE TO FIND IT
We Need to Grow Closer to Jesus Each Day	Acts 9:1-18	Pitcher, lemonade mix (sugarless), sugar, dry ice, a Bible	SS, p. 45
We Need to Grow Physically, Emotionally, and Spiritually	1 Peter 2:2	Photograph albums or videos of your children at different ages, tape measure, bathroom scale, Bible	CCQ, p. 75
We Need to Respect Each Other's Property	Ex. 20:15	Valuable family items	TC, p. 75
We Need to Treat His Name With Respect for It Represents God Who Is Holy	Ps. 99:3	Eggs, checkbook, a Bible	TC, p. 43
We Need to Try to Solve Our Differences and Forgive Before Our Attitude or Actions Become Wrongful	Matt. 5:23-26; 6:9-13	Basketballs, a bowl of M&Ms®, and a Bible	TC, p. 63
We Prove Who We Are When What We Do Reflects What We Say	James 1:22; 2:14-27	A bag of candy, a rope, and a Bible	HFN, p. 67
We Reap What We Sow	Gal. 6:7	Candy bar, Bible	IFN, p. 55
We Should Be on Guard Against "Wanting" for True Happiness Is Not Found in Things		Pennies or candy and a box	TC, p. 88
We Should Do What God Wants Even If We Don't Think We Can		A powerful fan, large sheet of light-weight black plastic, duct tape, and a flashlight	OTS, p. 86
We Should Live God-Centered Lives	Matt. 4:10	24 dominoes or small blocks for each family member, a Bible	TC, p. 29
We Shouldn't Value Possessions Over Everything Else	1 Tim. 6:7-8	Box is optional	CCQ, p. 18
When a Sheep Is Lost, the Shepherd Finds It		Shoe box, felt, pom pom balls	NTS, p. 58
When God Sent Jesus to Earth, God Chose Me	Luke 1:26-38; John 3:16; Matt. 14:23	Going to choose a Christmas tree or other special decoration, a Bible, and hot chocolate	HFN, p. 83

Family Night
TOOL CHEST

AN INTRODUCTION TO FAMILY NIGHTS
= IFN

BASIC CHRISTIAN BELIEFS
= BCB

CHRISTIAN CHARACTER QUALITIES
= CCQ

WISDOM LIFE SKILLS
= WLS

MONEY MATTERS FOR KIDS
= MMK

HOLIDAYS FAMILY NIGHT
= HFN

BIBLE STORIES FOR PRESCHOOLERS (OLD TESTAMENT)
= OTS

SIMPLE SCIENCE
= SS

BIBLE STORIES FOR PRESCHOOLERS (NEW TESTAMENT)
= NTS

TEN COMMANDMENTS
= TC

TOPIC	SCRIPTURE	WHAT YOU'LL NEED	WHERE TO FIND IT
When we accept Jesus' gift of salvation, we receive the Holy Spirit	John 3:5-8	1/4-full roll of toilet paper, a blow dryer, a dowel rod, a Bible	SS, p. 39
When We Focus on What We Don't Have, We Get Unhappy	1 Tim. 6:9-10; 1 Thes. 5:18; Phil. 4:11-13	A glass, water, paper, crayons, and a Bible	HFN, p. 71
When We See Something Wrong with the Way We Act We Should Fix It	James 1:22-24	Clothing, a large mirror, a Bible	NTS, p. 83
When We're Set Free from Sin, We Have the Freedom to Choose, and the Responsibility to Serve	Gal. 5:13-15	Candies, soft rope, and a Bible	HFN, p. 55
Wise Spending Means Getting Good Value for What We Buy	Luke 15:11-32	Money and a Bible	MMK, p. 97
With Help, Life Is a Lot Easier		Supplies to do the chore you choose	BCB, p. 101
Wolves in Sheeps' Clothing	Matt. 7:15-20	Ten paper sacks, a marker, ten small items, Bible	IFN, p. 97
Worrying Doesn't Change Anything		Board, inexpensive doorbell buzzer, a 9-volt battery, extra length of electrical wire, a large belt, assorted tools	CCQ, p. 37
You Can Choose to Obey or Not Obey, but You Can't Choose the Consequences	Josh. 6:12-17; 7:1-26	Bandana and a Bible	TC, p. 76
You Look Like the Person in Whose Image You Are Created		Paper roll, crayons, markers, pictures of your kids and of yourself as a child	BCB, p. 23

Welcome to the Family!

Heritage Builders

Helping You Build a Family of Faith

We hope you've enjoyed this book. Heritage Builders was founded in 1995 by three fathers with a passion for the next generation. As a new ministry of Focus on the Family, Heritage Builders strives to equip, train and motivate parents to become intentional about building a strong spiritual heritage.

It's quite a challenge for busy parents to find ways to build a spiritual foundation for their families—especially in a way they enjoy and understand. Through activities and participation, children can learn biblical truth in a way they can understand, enjoy—and *remember.*

Passing along a heritage of Christian faith to your family is a parent's highest calling. Heritage Builders' goal is to encourage and empower you in this great mission with practical resources and inspiring ideas that really work— and help your children develop a lasting love for God.

***

How To Reach Us

For more information, visit our Heritage Builders Web site! Log on to **www.heritagebuilders.com** to discover new resources, sample activities, and ideas to help you pass on a spiritual heritage. To request any of these resources, simply call Focus on the Family at 1-800-A-FAMILY (1-800-232-6459) or in Canada, call 1-800-661-9800. Or send your request to Focus on the Family, Colorado Springs, CO 80995. In Canada, write Focus on the Family, P.O. Box 9800, Stn. Terminal, Vancouver, B.C. V6B 4G3

To learn more about Focus on the Family or to find out if there is an associate office in your country, please visit www. family.org

We'd love to hear from you!

Try These Heritage Builders Resources!

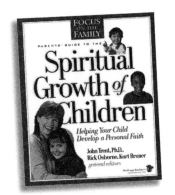

Parents' Guide to the Spiritual Growth of Children

Building a foundation of faith in your children can be easy–
and fun!–with help from the *Parents' Guide to the Spiritual Growth
of Children*. Through simple and practical advice,
this comprehensive guide shows you how to build a
spiritual training plan for your family and it explains
what to teach your children at different ages.

Bedtime Blessings

Strengthen the precious bond between you, your child and God by making
Bedtime Blessings a special part of your evenings together. From best-selling author John
Trent, Ph.D., and Heritage Builders, this book is filled with stories, activities and blessing
prayers to help you practice the biblical model of "blessing."

My Time With God

Send your child on an amazing adventure—a self-guided tour through God's Word! *My Time
With God* shows your 8- to 12-year-old how to get to know God regularly in exciting ways.
Through 150 days' worth of fun facts and mind-boggling trivia, prayer starters, and
interesting questions, your child will discover how awesome God really is!

The Singing Bible

Children ages 2 to 7 will love *The Singing Bible*, which sets the Bible to music with over
50 fun, sing-along songs! Lead your child through Scripture by using *The Singing Bible*
to introduce the story of Jonah, the Ten Commandments and more.
This is a fun, fast-paced journey kids will remember.

. . .

Visit our Heritage Builders Web Site! Log on to
www.heritagebuilders. com to discover new resources,
sample activities, and ideas to help you pass on a spiritual heritage.
To request any of these resources, simply call Focus on the Family at
1-800-A-FAMILY (1-800-232-6459) or in Canada, call 1-800-661-9800.
Or send your request to Focus on the Family, Colorado Springs, CO
80995. In Canada, Write Focus on the Family, P.O. Box 9800,
Stn. Terminal, Vancouver, B.C. V6B 4G3.

Heritage Builders™

Helping You Build a Family of Faith

Every family has a heritage—a spiritual, emotional, and social legacy passed from one generation to the next. There are four main areas we at Heritage Builders recommend parents consider as they plan to pass their faith to their children:

Family Fragrance

Every family's home has a fragrance. Heritage Builders encourages parents to create a home environment that fosters a sweet, Christ-centered AROMA of love through Affection, Respect, Order, Merriment, and Affirmation.

Family Traditions

Whether you pass down stories, beliefs and/or customs, traditions can help you establish a special identity for your family. Heritage Builders encourages parents to set special "milestones" for their children to help guide them and move them through their spiritual development.

Family Compass

Parents have the unique task of setting standards for normal, healthy living through their attitudes, actions and beliefs. Heritage Builders encourages parents to give their children the moral navigation tools they need to succeed on the roads of life.

Family Moments

Creating special, teachable moments with their children is one of a parent's most precious and sometimes, most difficult responsibilities. Heritage Builders encourages parents to capture little moments throughout the day to teach and impress values, beliefs, and biblical principles onto their children.

We look forward to standing alongside you as you seek to impart the Lord's care and wisdom onto the next generation—onto your children.

Heritage Builders™

Helping You Build a Family of Faith